May-Day

Ralph Waldo Emerson

Binker North

.

MAY-DAY

I

MAY-DAY.

Daughter of Heaven and Earth, coy Spring,
With sudden passion languishing,
Maketh all things softly smile,
Painteth pictures mile on mile,
Holds a cup with cowslip-wreaths,
Whence a smokeless incense breathes.
Girls are peeling the sweet willow,
Poplar white, and Gilead-tree,
And troops of boys
Shouting with whoop and hilloa,
And hip, hip three times three.
The air is full of whistlings bland;
What was that I heard
Out of the hazy land?
Harp of the wind, or song of bird,
Or clapping of shepherd's hands,
Or vagrant booming of the air,
Voice of a meteor lost in day?
Such tidings of the starry sphere
Can this elastic air convey.
Or haply 't was the cannonade

Of the pent and darkened lake,
Cooled by the pendent mountain's shade,
Whose deeps, till beams of noonday break,
Afflicted moan, and latest hold
Even unto May the iceberg cold.
Was it a squirrel's pettish bark,
Or clarionet of jay? or hark,
Where yon wedged line the Nestor leads,
Steering north with raucous cry
Through tracts and provinces of sky,
Every night alighting down
In new landscapes of romance,
Where darkling feed the clamorous clans
By lonely lakes to men unknown.
Come the tumult whence it will,
Voice of sport, or rush of wings,
It is a sound, it is a token
That the marble sleep is broken,
And a change has passed on things.
Beneath the calm, within the light,
A hid unruly appetite
Of swifter life, a surer hope,
Strains every sense to larger scope,
Impatient to anticipate
The halting steps of aged Fate.
Slow grows the palm, too slow the pearl:
When Nature falters, fain would zeal
Grasp the felloes of her wheel,
And grasping give the orbs another whirl.
Turn swiftlier round, O tardy ball!
And sun this frozen side,
Bring hither back the robin's call,
Bring back the tulip's pride.

Why chidest thou the tardy Spring?
The hardy bunting does not chide;
The blackbirds make the maples ring
With social cheer and jubilee;
The redwing flutes his o-ka-lee,
The robins know the melting snow;
The sparrow meek, prophetic-eyed,
Her nest beside the snow-drift weaves,
Secure the osier yet will hide
Her callow brood in mantling leaves;
And thou, by science all undone,
Why only must thy reason fail
To see the southing of the sun?
As we thaw frozen flesh with snow,
So Spring will not, foolish fond,
Mix polar night with tropic glow,
Nor cloy us with unshaded sun,
Nor wanton skip with bacchic dance,
But she has the temperance
Of the gods, whereof she is one,--
Masks her treasury of heat
Under east-winds crossed with sleet.
Plants and birds and humble creatures
Well accept her rule austere;
Titan-born, to hardy natures
Cold is genial and dear.
As Southern wrath to Northern right
Is but straw to anthracite;
As in the day of sacrifice,
When heroes piled the pyre,
The dismal Massachusetts ice
Burned more than others' fire,
So Spring guards with surface cold

The garnered heat of ages old:
Hers to sow the seed of bread,
That man and all the kinds be fed;
And, when the sunlight fills the hours,
Dissolves the crust, displays the flowers.
The world rolls round,--mistrust it not,--
Befalls again what once befell;
All things return, both sphere and mote,
And I shall hear my bluebird's note,
And dream the dream of Auburn dell.
When late I walked, in earlier days,
All was stiff and stark;
Knee-deep snows choked all the ways,
In the sky no spark;
Firm-braced I sought my ancient woods,
Struggling through the drifted roads;
The whited desert knew me not,
Snow-ridges masked each darling spot;
The summer dells, by genius haunted,
One arctic moon had disenchanted.
All the sweet secrets therein hid
By Fancy, ghastly spells undid.
Eldest mason, Frost, had piled,
With wicked ingenuity,
Swift cathedrals in the wild;
The piny hosts were sheeted ghosts
In the star-lit minster aisled.
I found no joy: the icy wind
Might rule the forest to his mind.
Who would freeze in frozen brakes?
Back to books and sheltered home,
And wood-fire flickering on the walls,
To hear, when, 'mid our talk and games,

Without the baffled north-wind calls.
But soft! a sultry morning breaks;
The cowslips make the brown brook gay;
A happier hour, a longer day.
Now the sun leads in the May,
Now desire of action wakes,
And the wish to roam.
The caged linnet in the Spring
Hearkens for the choral glee,
When his fellows on the wing
Migrate from the Southern Sea;
When trellised grapes their flowers unmask,
And the new-born tendrils twine,
The old wine darkling in the cask
Feels the bloom on the living vine,
And bursts the hoops at hint of Spring:
And so, perchance, in Adam's race,
Of Eden's bower some dream-like trace
Survived the Flight, and swam the Flood,
And wakes the wish in youngest blood
To tread the forfeit Paradise,
And feed once more the exile's eyes;
And ever when the happy child
In May beholds the blooming wild,
And hears in heaven the bluebird sing,
"Onward," he cries, "your baskets bring,--
In the next field is air more mild,
And o'er yon hazy crest is Eden's balmier Spring."
Not for a regiment's parade,
Nor evil laws or rulers made,
Blue Walden rolls its cannonade,
But for a lofty sign
Which the Zodiac threw,

That the bondage-days are told,
And waters free as winds shall flow.
Lo! how all the tribes combine
To rout the flying foe.
See, every patriot oak-leaf throws
His elfin length upon the snows,
Not idle, since the leaf all day
Draws to the spot the solar ray,
Ere sunset quarrying inches down,
And half-way to the mosses brown;
While the grass beneath the rime
Has hints of the propitious time,
And upward pries and perforates
Through the cold slab a thousand gates,
Till green lances peering through
Bend happy in the welkin blue.
April cold with dropping rain
Willows and lilacs brings again,
The whistle of returning birds,
And trumpet-lowing of the herds.
The scarlet maple-keys betray
What potent blood hath modest May;
What fiery force the earth renews,
The wealth of forms, the flush of hues;
Joy shed in rosy waves abroad
Flows from the heart of Love, the Lord.
Hither rolls the storm of heat;
I feel its finer billows beat
Like a sea which me infolds;
Heat with viewless fingers moulds,
Swells, and mellows, and matures,
Paints, and flavours, and allures,
Bird and brier inly warms,

Still enriches and transforms,
Gives the reed and lily length,
Adds to oak and oxen strength,
Boils the world in tepid lakes,
Burns the world, yet burnt remakes;
Enveloping heat, enchanted robe,
Wraps the daisy and the globe,
Transforming what it doth infold,
Life out of death, new out of old,
Painting fawns' and leopards' fells,
Seethes the gulf-encrimsoning shells,
Fires garden with a joyful blaze
Of tulips in the morning's rays.
The dead log touched bursts into leaf,
The wheat-blade whispers of the sheaf.
What god is this imperial Heat,
Earth's prime secret, sculpture's seat?
Doth it bear hidden in its heart
Water-line patterns of all art,
All figures, organs, hues, and graces?
Is it Daedalus? is it Love?
Or walks in mask almighty Jove,
And drops from Power's redundant horn
All seeds of beauty to be born?
Where shall we keep the holiday,
And duly greet the entering May?
Too strait and low our cottage doors,
And all unmeet our carpet floors;
Nor spacious court, nor monarch's hall,
Suffice to hold the festival.
Up and away! where haughty woods
Front the liberated floods:
We will climb the broad-backed hills,

Hear the uproar of their joy;
We will mark the leaps and gleams
Of the new-delivered streams,
And the murmuring rivers of sap
Mount in the pipes of the trees,
Giddy with day, to the topmost spire,
Which for a spike of tender green
Bartered its powdery cap;
And the colours of joy in the bird,
And the love in its carol heard,
Frog and lizard in holiday coats,
And turtle brave in his golden spots;
We will hear the tiny roar
Of the insects evermore,
While cheerful cries of crag and plain
Reply to the thunder of river and main.
As poured the flood of the ancient sea
Spilling over mountain chains,
Bending forests as bends the sedge,
Faster flowing o'er the plains,--
A world-wide wave with a foaming edge
That rims the running silver sheet,--
So pours the deluge of the heat
Broad northward o'er the land,
Painting artless paradises,
Drugging herbs with Syrian spices,
Fanning secret fires which glow
In columbine and clover-blow,
Climbing the northern zones,
Where a thousand pallid towns
Lie like cockles by the main,
Or tented armies on a plain.
The million-handed sculptor moulds

Quaintest bud and blossom folds,
The million-handed painter pours
Opal hues and purple dye;
Azaleas flush the island floors,
And the tints of heaven reply.
Wreaths for the May! for happy Spring
To-day shall all her dowry bring,
The love of kind, the joy, the grace,
Hymen of element and race,
Knowing well to celebrate
With song and hue and star and state,
With tender light and youthful cheer,
The spousals of the new-born year.
Lo Love's inundation poured
Over space and race abroad!
Spring is strong and virtuous,
Broad-sowing, cheerful, plenteous,
Quickening underneath the mould
Grains beyond the price of gold.
So deep and large her bounties are,
That one broad, long midsummer day
Shall to the planet overpay
The ravage of a year of war.
Drug the cup, thou butler sweet,
And send the nectar round;
The feet that slid so long on sleet
Are glad to feel the ground.
Fill and saturate each kind
With good according to its mind,
Fill each kind and saturate
With good agreeing with its fate,
Willow and violet, maiden and man.
The bitter-sweet, the haunting air,

Creepeth, bloweth everywhere;
It preys on all, all prey on it,
Blooms in beauty, thinks in wit,
Stings the strong with enterprise,
Makes travellers long for Indian skies,
And where it comes this courier fleet
Fans in all hearts expectance sweet,
As if to-morrow should redeem
The vanished rose of evening's dream.
By houses lies a fresher green,
On men and maids a ruddier mien,
As if time brought a new relay
Of shining virgins every May,
And Summer came to ripen maids
To a beauty that not fades.
The ground-pines wash their rusty green,
The maple-tops their crimson tint,
On the soft path each track is seen,
The girl's foot leaves its neater print.
The pebble loosened from the frost
Asks of the urchin to be tost.
In flint and marble beats a heart,
The kind Earth takes her children's part,
The green lane is the school-boy's friend,
Low leaves his quarrel apprehend,
The fresh ground loves his top and ball,
The air rings jocund to his call,
The brimming brook invites a leap,
He dives the hollow, climbs the steep.
The youth reads omens where he goes,
And speaks all languages the rose.
The wood-fly mocks with tiny noise
The far halloo of human voice;

The perfumed berry on the spray
Smacks of faint memories far away.
A subtle chain of countless rings
The next unto the farthest brings,
And, striving to be man, the worm
Mounts through all the spires of form.
I saw the bud-crowned Spring go forth,
Stepping daily onward north
To greet staid ancient cavaliers
Filing single in stately train.
And who, and who are the travellers?
They were Night and Day, and Day and Night,
Pilgrims wight with step forthright.
I saw the Days deformed and low,
Short and bent by cold and snow;
The merry Spring threw wreaths on them,
Flower-wreaths gay with bud and bell;
Many a flower and many a gem,
They were refreshed by the smell,
They shook the snow from hats and shoon,
They put their April raiment on;
And those eternal forms,
Unhurt by a thousand storms,
Shot up to the height of the sky again,
And danced as merrily as young men.
I saw them mask their awful glance
Sidewise meek in gossamer lids;
And to speak my thought if none forbids.
It was as if the eternal gods,
Tired of their starry periods,
Hid their majesty in cloth
Woven of tulips and painted moth.
On carpets green the maskers march

Below May's well-appointed arch,
Each star, each god, each grace amain,
Every joy and virtue speed,
Marching duly in her train,
And fainting Nature at her need
Is made whole again.
'T was the vintage-day of field and wood,
When magic wine for bards is brewed;
Every tree and stem and chink
Gushed with syrup to the brink.
The air stole into the streets of towns,
And betrayed the fund of joy
To the high-school and medalled boy:
On from hall to chamber ran,
From youth to maid, from boy to man,
To babes, and to old eyes as well.
'Once more,' the old man cried, 'ye clouds,
Airy turrets purple-piled,
Which once my infancy beguiled,
Beguile me with the wonted spell.
I know ye skilful to convoy
The total freight of hope and joy
Into rude and homely nooks,
Shed mocking lustres on shelf of books,
On farmer's byre, on meadow-pipes,
Or on a pool of dancing chips.
I care not if the pomps you show
Be what they soothfast appear,
Or if yon realms in sunset glow
Be bubbles of the atmosphere.
And if it be to you allowed
To fool me with a shining cloud,
So only new griefs are consoled

By new delights, as old by old,
Frankly I will be your guest,
Count your change and cheer the best.
The world hath overmuch of pain,--
If Nature give me joy again,
Of such deceit I'll not complain.'
Ah! well I mind the calendar,
Faithful through a thousand years,
Of the painted race of flowers,
Exact to days, exact to hours,
Counted on the spacious dial
Yon broidered zodiac girds.
I know the pretty almanac
Of the punctual coming-back,
On their due days, of the birds.
I marked them yestermorn,
A flock of finches darting
Beneath the crystal arch,
Piping, as they flew, a march,--
Belike the one they used in parting
Last year from yon oak or larch;
Dusky sparrows in a crowd,
Diving, darting northward free,
Suddenly betook them all,
Every one to his hole in the wall,
Or to his niche in the apple-tree.
I greet with joy the choral trains
Fresh from palms and Cuba's canes.
Best gems of Nature's cabinet,
With dews of tropic morning wet,
Beloved of children, bards, and Spring,
O birds, your perfect virtues bring,
Your song, your forms, your rhythmic flight,

Your manners for the heart's delight,
Nestle in hedge, or barn, or roof,
Here weave your chamber weather-proof,
Forgive our harms, and condescend
To man, as to a lubber friend,
And, generous, teach his awkward race
Courage, and probity, and grace!
Poets praise that hidden wine
Hid in milk we drew
At the barrier of Time,
When our life was new.
We had eaten fairy fruit,
We were quick from head to foot,
All the forms we look on shone
As with diamond dews thereon.
What cared we for costly joys,
The Museum's far-fetched toys?
Gleam of sunshine on the wall
Poured a deeper cheer than all
The revels of the Carnival.
We a pine-grove did prefer
To a marble theatre,
Could with gods on mallows dine,
Nor cared for spices or for wine.
Wreaths of mist and rainbow spanned,
Arch on arch, the grimmest land;
Whistle of a woodland bird
Made the pulses dance,
Note of horn in valleys heard
Filled the region with romance.
None can tell how sweet,
How virtuous, the morning air;
Every accent vibrates well;

Not alone the wood-bird's call,
Or shouting boys that chase their ball,
Pass the height of minstrel skill,
But the ploughman's thoughtless cry,
Lowing oxen, sheep that bleat,
And the joiner's hammer-beat,
Softened are above their will.
All grating discords melt,
No dissonant note is dealt,
And though thy voice be shrill
Like rasping file on steel,
Such is the temper of the air,
Echo waits with art and care,
And will the faults of song repair.
So by remote Superior Lake,
And by resounding Mackinac,
When northern storms and forests shake,
And billows on the long beach break,
The artful Air doth separate
Note by note all sounds that grate,
Smothering in her ample breast
All but godlike words,
Reporting to the happy ear
Only purified accords.
Strangely wrought from barking waves,
Soft music daunts the Indian braves,--
Convent-chanting which the child
Hears pealing from the panther's cave
And the impenetrable wild.
One musician is sure,
His wisdom will not fail,
He has not tasted wine impure,
Nor bent to passion frail.

Age cannot cloud his memory,
Nor grief untune his voice,
Ranging down the ruled scale
From tone of joy to inward wail,
Tempering the pitch of all
In his windy cave.
He all the fables knows,
And in their causes tells,--
Knows Nature's rarest moods,
Ever on her secret broods.
The Muse of men is coy,
Oft courted will not come;
In palaces and market squares
Entreated, she is dumb;
But my minstrel knows and tells
The counsel of the gods,
Knows of Holy Book the spells,
Knows the law of Night and Day,
And the heart of girl and boy,
The tragic and the gay,
And what is writ on Table Round
Of Arthur and his peers,
What sea and land discoursing say
In sidereal years.
He renders all his lore
In numbers wild as dreams,
Modulating all extremes,--
What the spangled meadow saith
To the children who have faith;
Only to children children sing,
Only to youth will spring be spring.
Who is the Bard thus magnified?
When did he sing, and where abide?

Chief of song where poets feast
Is the wind-harp which thou seest
In the casement at my side.
AEolian harp,
How strangely wise thy strain!
Gay for youth, gay for youth,
(Sweet is art, but sweeter truth,)
In the hall at summer eve
Fate and Beauty skilled to weave.
From the eager opening strings
Rung loud and bold the song.
Who but loved the wind-harp's note?
How should not the poet doat
On its mystic tongue,
With its primeval memory,
Reporting what old minstrels said
Of Merlin locked the harp within,--
Merlin paying the pain of sin,
Pent in a dungeon made of air,--
And some attain his voice to hear,
Words of pain and cries of fear,
But pillowed all on melody,
As fits the griefs of bards to be.
And what if that all-echoing shell,
Which thus the buried Past can tell,
Should rive the Future, and reveal
What his dread folds would fain conceal?
It shares the secret of the earth,
And of the kinds that owe her birth.
Speaks not of self that mystic tone,
But of the Overgods alone:
It trembles to the cosmic breath,--
As it heareth, so it saith;

Obeying meek the primal Cause,
It is the tongue of mundane laws:
And this, at least, I dare affirm,
Since genius too has bound and term,
There is no bard in all the choir,
Not Homer's self, the poet sire,
Wise Milton's odes of pensive pleasure,
Or Shakspeare, whom no mind can measure,
Nor Collins' verse of tender pain,
Nor Byron's clarion of disdain,
Scott, the delight of generous boys,
Or Wordsworth, Pan's recording voice,--
Not one of all can put in verse,
Or to this presence could rehearse,
The sights and voices ravishing
The boy knew on the hills in Spring,
When pacing through the oaks he heard
Sharp queries of the sentry-bird,
The heavy grouse's sudden whirr,
The rattle of the kingfisher;
Saw bonfires of the harlot flies
In the lowland, when day dies;
Or marked, benighted and forlorn,
The first far signal-fire of morn.
These syllables that Nature spoke,
And the thoughts that in him woke,
Can adequately utter none
Save to his ear the wind-harp lone.
And best can teach its Delphian chord
How Nature to the soul is moored,
If once again that silent string,
As erst it wont, would thrill and ring.
Not long ago, at eventide,

It seemed, so listening, at my side
A window rose, and, to say sooth,
I looked forth on the fields of youth:
I saw fair boys bestriding steeds,
I knew their forms in fancy weeds,
Long, long concealed by sundering fates,
Mates of my youth,--yet not my mates,
Stronger and bolder far than I,
With grace, with genius, well attired,
And then as now from far admired,
Followed with love
They knew not of,
With passion cold and shy.
O joy, for what recoveries rare!
Renewed, I breathe Elysian air,
See youth's glad mates in earliest bloom,--
Break not my dream, obtrusive tomb!
Or teach thou, Spring! the grand recoil
Of life resurgent from the soil
Wherein was dropped the mortal spoil.
Soft on the south-wind sleeps the haze!
So on thy broad mystic van
Lie the opal-coloured days,
And waft the miracle to man.
Soothsayer of the eldest gods,
Repairer of what harms betide,
Revealer of the inmost powers
Prometheus proffered, Jove denied;
Disclosing treasures more than true,
Or in what far to-morrow due;
Speaking by the tongues of flowers,
By the ten-tongued laurel speaking,
Singing by the oriole songs,

Heart of bird the man's heart seeking;
Whispering hints of treasure hid
Under Morn's unlifted lid,
Islands looming just beyond
The dim horizon's utmost bound;--
Who can, like thee, our rags upbraid,
Or taunt us with our hope decayed?
Or who like thee persuade,
Making the splendour of the air,
The morn and sparkling dew, a snare?
Or who resent
Thy genius, wiles, and blandishment?
There is no orator prevails
To beckon or persuade
Like thee the youth or maid:
Thy birds, thy songs, thy brooks, thy gales,
Thy blooms, thy kinds,
Thy echoes in the wilderness,
Soothe pain, and age, and love's distress,
Fire fainting will, and build heroic minds.
For thou, O Spring! canst renovate
All that high God did first create.
Be still his arm and architect,
Rebuild the ruin, mend defect;
Chemist to vamp old worlds with new,
Coat sea and sky with heavenlier blue,
New-tint the plumage of the birds,
And slough decay from grazing herds,
Sweep ruins from the scarped mountain,
Cleanse the torrent at the fountain,
Purge alpine air by towns defiled,
Bring to fair mother fairer child,
Not less renew the heart and brain,

Scatter the sloth, wash out the stain,
Make the aged eye sun-clear,
To parting soul bring grandeur near.
Under gentle types, my Spring
Masks the might of Nature's king,
An energy that searches thorough
From Chaos to the dawning morrow;
Into all our human plight,
The soul's pilgrimage and flight;
In city or in solitude,
Step by step, lifts bad to good,
Without halting, without rest,
Lifting Better up to Best;
Planting seeds of knowledge pure,
Through earth to ripen, through heaven endure.

THE ADIRONDACS.

A JOURNAL.

DEDICATED TO MY FELLOW-TRAVELLERS IN AUGUST, 1858.

Wise and polite,--and if I drew
Their several portraits, you would own
Chaucer had no such worthy crew,
Nor Boccace in Decameron.
We crossed Champlain to Keeseville with our friends,
Thence, in strong country carts, rode up the forks
Of the Ausable stream, intent to reach
The Adirondac lakes. At Martin's Beach
We chose our boats; each man a boat and guide,--
Ten men, ten guides, our company all told.
Next morn, we swept with oars the Saranac,
With skies of benediction, to Round Lake,

Where all the sacred mountains drew around us,
Tahawus, Seaward, MacIntyre, Baldhead,
And other Titans without muse or name.
Pleased with these grand companions, we glide on,
Instead of flowers, crowned with a wreath of hills,
And made our distance wider, boat from boat,
As each would hear the oracle alone.
By the bright morn the gay flotilla slid
Through files of flags that gleamed like bayonets,
Through gold-moth-haunted beds of pickerel-flower,
Through scented banks of lilies white and gold,
Where the deer feeds at night, the teal by day,
On through the Upper Saranac, and up
Pere Raquette stream, to a small tortuous pass
Winding through grassy shallows in and out,
Two creeping miles of rushes, pads, and sponge,
To Follansbee Water, and the Lake of Loons.
Northward the length of Follansbee we rowed,
Under low mountains, whose unbroken ridge
Ponderous with beechen forest sloped the shore.
A pause and council: then, where near the head
On the east a bay makes inward to the land
Between two rocky arms, we climb the bank,
And in the twilight of the forest noon
Wield the first axe these echoes ever heard.
We cut young trees to make our poles and thwarts,
Barked the white spruce to weatherfend the roof,
Then struck a light, and kindled the camp-fire.
The wood was sovran with centennial trees,--
Oak, cedar, maple, poplar, beech and fir,
Linden and spruce. In strict society
Three conifers, white, pitch, and Norway pine,
Five-leaved, three-leaved, and two-leaved, grew thereby.

Our patron pine was fifteen feet in girth,
The maple eight, beneath its shapely tower.
'Welcome!' the wood god murmured through the leaves,--
'Welcome, though late, unknowing, yet known to me.'
Evening drew on; stars peeped through maple-boughs,
Which o'erhung, like a cloud, our camping fire.
Decayed millennial trunks, like moonlight flecks,
Lit with phosphoric crumbs the forest floor.
Ten scholars, wonted to lie warm and soft
In well-hung chambers daintily bestowed,
Lie here on hemlock-boughs, like Sacs and Sioux,
And greet unanimous the joyful change.
So fast will Nature acclimate her sons,
Though late returning to her pristine ways.
Off soundings, seamen do not suffer cold;
And, in the forest, delicate clerks, unbrowned,
Sleep on the fragrant brush, as on down-beds.
Up with the dawn, they fancied the light air
That circled freshly in their forest dress
Made them to boys again. Happier that they
Slipped off their pack of duties, leagues behind,
At the first mounting of the giant stairs.
No placard on these rocks warned to the polls,
No door-bell heralded a visitor,
No courier waits, no letter came or went,
Nothing was ploughed, or reaped, or bought, or sold;
The frost might glitter, it would blight no crop,
The falling rain will spoil no holiday.
We were made freemen of the forest laws,
All dressed, like Nature, fit for her own ends,
Essaying nothing she cannot perform.
In Adirondac lakes,
At morn or noon, the guide rows bareheaded:

Shoes, flannel shirt, and kersey trousers make
His brief toilette: at night, or in the rain,
He dons a surcoat which he doffs at morn:
A paddle in the right hand, or an oar,
And in the left, a gun, his needful arms.
By turns we praised the stature of our guides,
Their rival strength and suppleness, their skill
To row, to swim, to shoot, to build a camp,
To climb a lofty stem, clean without boughs
Full fifty feet, and bring the eaglet down:
Temper to face wolf, bear, or catamount,
And wit to track or take him in his lair.
Sound, ruddy men, frolic and innocent,
In winter, lumberers; in summer, guides;
Their sinewy arms pull at the oar untired
Three times ten thousand strokes, from morn to eve.
Look to yourselves, ye polished gentlemen!
No city airs or arts pass current here.
Your rank is all reversed: let men of cloth
Bow to the stalwart churls in overalls:
They are the doctors of the wilderness,
And we the low-prized laymen.
In sooth, red flannel is a saucy test
Which few can put on with impunity.
What make you, master, fumbling at the oar?
Will you catch crabs? Truth tries pretension here.
The sallow knows the basket-maker's thumb;
The oar, the guide's. Dare you accept the tasks
He shall impose, to find a spring, trap foxes,
Tell the sun's time, determine the true north,
Or stumbling on through vast self-similar woods
To thread by night the nearest way to camp?
Ask you, how went the hours?

All day we swept the lake, searched every cove,
North from Camp Maple, south to Osprey Bay,
Watching when the loud dogs should drive in deer,
Or whipping its rough surface for a trout;
Or bathers, diving from the rock at noon;
Challenging Echo by our guns and cries;
Or listening to the laughter of the loon;
Or, in the evening twilight's latest red,
Beholding the procession of the pines;
Or, later yet, beneath a lighted jack,
In the boat's bows, a silent night-hunter
Stealing with paddle to the feeding-grounds
Of the red deer, to aim at a square mist.
Hark to that muffled roar! a tree in the woods
Is fallen: but hush! it has not scared the buck
Who stands astonished at the meteor light,
Then turns to bound away,--is it too late?
Sometimes we tried our rifles at a mark,
Six rods, sixteen, twenty, or forty-five;
Sometimes our wits at sally and retort,
With laughter sudden as the crack of rifle;
Or parties scaled the near acclivities
Competing seekers of a rumoured lake,
Whose unauthenticated waves we named
Lake Probability,--our carbuncle,
Long sought, not found.
Two Doctors in the camp
Dissected the slain deer, weighed the trout's brain,
Captured the lizard, salamander, shrew,
Crab, mice, snail, dragon-fly, minnow, and moth;
Insatiate skill in water or in air
Waved the scoop-net, and nothing came amiss;
The while, one leaden pot of alcohol

Gave an impartial tomb to all the kinds.
Not less the ambitious botanist sought plants,
Orchis and gentian, fern, and long whip-scirpus,
Rosy polygonum, lake-margin's pride,
Hypnum and hydnum, mushroom, sponge, and moss,
Or harebell nodding in the gorge of falls.
Above, the eagle flew, the osprey screamed,
The raven croaked, owls hooted, the woodpecker
Loud hammered, and the heron rose in the swamp.
As water poured through the hollows of the hills
To feed this wealth of lakes and rivulets,
So Nature shed all beauty lavishly
From her redundant horn.
Lords of this realm,
Bounded by dawn and sunset, and the day
Rounded by hours where each outdid the last
In miracles of pomp, we must be proud,
As if associates of the sylvan gods.
We seemed the dwellers of the zodiac,
So pure the Alpine element we breathed,
So light, so lofty pictures came and went.
We trode on air, contemned the distant town,
Its timorous ways, big trifles, and we planned
That we should build, hard-by, a spacious lodge,
And how we should come hither with our sons,
Hereafter,--willing they, and more adroit.
Hard fare, hard bed, and comic misery,--
The midge, the blue-fly, and the mosquito
Painted our necks, hands, ankles, with red bands:
But, on the second day, we heed them not,
Nay, we saluted them Auxiliaries,
Whom earlier we had chid with spiteful names.
For who defends our leafy tabernacle

From bold intrusion of the travelling crowd,--
Who but the midge, mosquito, and the fly,
Which past endurance sting the tender cit,
But which we learn to scatter with a smudge,
Or baffle by a veil, or slight by scorn?
Our foaming ale we drunk from hunters' pans,
Ale, and a sup of wine. Our steward gave
Venison and trout, potatoes, beans, wheat-bread;
All ate like abbots, and, if any missed
Their wonted convenance, cheerly hid the loss
With hunters' appetite and peals of mirth.
And Stillman, our guides' guide, and Commodore,
Crusoe, Crusader, Pius AEneas, said aloud,
"Chronic dyspepsia never came from eating
Food indigestible":--then murmured some,
Others applauded him who spoke the truth.
Nor doubt but visitings of graver thought
Checked in these souls the turbulent heyday
'Mid all the hints and glories of the home.
For who can tell what sudden privacies
Were sought and found, amid the hue and cry
Of scholars furloughed from their tasks, and let
Into this Oreads' fended Paradise,
As chapels in the city's thoroughfares,
Whither gaunt Labour slips to wipe his brow,
And meditate a moment on Heaven's rest.
Judge with what sweet surprises Nature spoke
To each apart, lifting her lovely shows
To spiritual lessons pointed home.
And as through dreams in watches of the night,
So through all creatures in their form and ways
Some mystic hint accosts the vigilant,
Not clearly voiced, but waking a new sense

27

Inviting to new knowledge, one with old.
Hark to that petulant chirp! what ails the warbler?
Mark his capricious ways to draw the eye.
Now soar again. What wilt thou, restless bird,
Seeking in that chaste blue a bluer light,
Thirsting in that pure for a purer sky?
And presently the sky is changed; O world!
What pictures and what harmonies are thine!
The clouds are rich and dark, the air serene,
So like the soul of me, what if't were me?
A melancholy better than all mirth.
Comes the sweet sadness at the retrospect,
Or at the foresight of obscurer years?
Like yon slow-sailing cloudy promontory,
Whereon the purple iris dwells in beauty
Superior to all its gaudy skirts.
And, that no day of life may lack romance,
The spiritual stars rise nightly, shedding down
A private beam into each several heart.
Daily the bending skies solicit man,
The seasons chariot him from this exile,
The rainbow hours bedeck his glowing chair,
The storm-winds urge the heavy weeks along,
Suns haste to set, that so remoter lights
Beckon the wanderer to his vaster home.
With a vermilion pencil mark the day
When of our little fleet three cruising skiffs
Entering Big Tupper, bound for the foaming Falls
Of loud Bog River, suddenly confront
Two of our mates returning with swift oars.
One held a printed journal waving high
Caught from a late-arriving traveller,
Big with great news, and shouted the report

For which the world had waited, now firm fact,
Of the wire-cable laid beneath the sea,
And landed on our coast, and pulsating
With ductile fire. Loud, exulting cries
From boat to boat, and to the echoes round,
Greet the glad miracle. Thought's new-found path
Shall supplement henceforth all trodden ways,
Match God's equator with a zone of art,
And lift man's public action to a height
Worthy the enormous clouds of witnesses,
When linked hemispheres attest his deed.
We have few moments in the longest life
Of such delight and wonder as there grew,--
Nor yet unsuited to that solitude:
A burst of joy, as if we told the fact
To ears intelligent; as if gray rock
And cedar grove and cliff and lake should know
This feat of wit, this triumph of mankind;
As if we men were talking in a vein
Of sympathy so large, that ours was theirs,
And a prime end of the most subtle element
Were fairly reached at last. Wake, echoing caves!
Bend nearer, faint day-moon! Yon thundertops,
Let them hear well! 't is theirs as much as ours.
A spasm throbbing through the pedestals
Of Alp and Andes, isle and continent,
Urging astonished Chaos with a thrill
To be a brain, or serve the brain of man.
The lightning has run masterless too long;
He must to school, and learn his verb and noun,
And teach his nimbleness to earn his wage,
Spelling with guided tongue man's messages
Shot through the weltering pit of the salt sea.

And yet I marked, even in the manly joy
Of our great-hearted Doctor in his boat,
(Perchance I erred,) a shade of discontent;
Or was it for mankind a generous shame,
As of a luck not quite legitimate,
Since fortune snatched from wit the lion's part?
Was it a college pique of town and gown,
As one within whose memory it burned
That not academicians, but some lout,
Found ten years since the Californian gold?
And now, again, a hungry company
Of traders, led by corporate sons of trade,
Perversely borrowing from the shop the tools
Of science, not from the philosophers,
Had won the brightest laurel of all time.
'Twas always thus, and will be; hand and head
Are ever rivals: but, though this be swift,
The other slow,--this the Prometheus,
And that the Jove,--yet, howsoever hid,
It was from Jove the other stole his fire,
And, without Jove, the good had never been.
It is not Iroquois or cannibals,
But ever the free race with front sublime,
And these instructed by their wisest too,
Who do the feat, and lift humanity.
Let not him mourn who best entitled was,
Nay, mourn not one: let him exult,
Yea, plant the tree that bears best apples, plant,
And water it with wine, nor watch askance
Whether thy sons or strangers eat the fruit:
Enough that mankind eat, and are refreshed.
We flee away from cities, but we bring
The best of cities with us, these learned classifiers,

Men knowing what they seek, armed eyes of experts.
We praise the guide, we praise the forest life;
But will we sacrifice our dear-bought lore
Of books and arts and trained experiment,
Or count the Sioux a match for Agassiz?
O no, not we! Witness the shout that shook
Wild Tupper Lake; witness the mute all-hail
The joyful traveller gives, when on the verge
Of craggy Indian wilderness he hears
From a log-cabin stream Beethoven's notes
On the piano, played with master's hand.
'Well done!' he cries; 'the bear is kept at bay,
The lynx, the rattlesnake, the flood, the fire;
All the fierce enemies, ague, hunger, cold,
This thin spruce roof, this clayed log-wall,
This wild plantation will suffice to chase.
Now speed the gay celerities of art,
What in the desert was impossible
Within four walls is possible again,--
Culture and libraries, mysteries of skill,
Traditioned fame of masters, eager strife
Of keen competing youths, joined or alone
To outdo each other, and extort applause.
Mind wakes a new-born giant from her sleep.
Twirl the old wheels? Time takes fresh start again
On for a thousand years of genius more.'
The holidays were fruitful, but must end;
One August evening had a cooler breath;
Into each mind intruding duties crept;
Under the cinders burned the fires of home;
Nay, letters found us in our paradise;
So in the gladness of the new event
We struck our camp, and left the happy hills.

The fortunate star that rose on us sank not;
The prodigal sunshine rested on the land,
The rivers gambolled onward to the sea,
And Nature, the inscrutable and mute,
Permitted on her infinite repose
Almost a smile to steal to cheer her sons,
As if one riddle of the Sphinx were guessed.

OCCASIONAL AND MISCELLANEOUS PIECES.

BRAHMA.
If the red slayer think he slays,
Or if the slain think he is slain,
They know well the subtle ways
I keep, and pass, and turn again.
Far or forgot to me is near;
Shadow and sunlight are the same;
The vanquished gods to me appear;
And one to me are shame and fame.
They reckon ill who leave me out;
When me they fly, I am the wings;
I am the doubter and the doubt,
And I the hymn the Brahmin sings.
The strong gods pine for my abode,
And pine in vain the sacred Seven;
But thou, meek lover of the good!
Find me, and turn thy back on heaven.
NEMESIS.
Already blushes in thy cheek
The bosom-thought which thou must speak;
The bird, how far it haply roam
By cloud or isle, is flying home;
The maiden fears, and fearing runs

Into the charmed snare she shuns;
And every man, in love or pride,
Of his fate is never wide.
Will a woman's fan the ocean smooth?
Or prayers the stony Parcae sooth,
Or coax the thunder from its mark?
Or tapers light the chaos dark?
In spite of Virtue and the Muse,
Nemesis will have her dues,
And all our struggles and our toils
Tighter wind the giant coils.
FATE.
Deep in the man sits fast his fate
To mould his fortunes mean or great:
Unknown to Cromwell as to me
Was Cromwell's measure or degree;
Unknown to him, as to his horse,
If he than his groom be better or worse.
He works, plots, fights, in rude affairs,
With squires, lords, kings, his craft compares,
Till late he learned, through doubt and fear,
Broad England harboured not his peer:
Obeying Time, the last to own
The Genius from its cloudy throne.
For the prevision is allied
Unto the thing so signified;
Or say, the foresight that awaits
Is the same Genius that creates.
FREEDOM.
Once I wished I might rehearse
Freedom's paean in my verse,
That the slave who caught the strain
Should throb until he snapped his chain.

But the Spirit said, 'Not so;
Speak it not, or speak it low;
Name not lightly to be said,
Gift too precious to be prayed,
Passion not to be expressed
But by heaving of the breast:
Yet,--wouldst thou the mountain find
Where this deity is shrined,
Who gives to seas and sunset skies
Their unspent beauty of surprise,
And, when it lists him, waken can
Brute or savage into man;
Or, if in thy heart he shine,
Blends the starry fates with thine,
Draws angels nigh to dwell with thee,
And makes thy thoughts archangels be;
Freedom's secret wilt thou know?--
Counsel not with flesh and blood;
Loiter not for cloak or food;
Right thou feelest, rush to do.'

ODE SUNG IN THE TOWN HALL, CONCORD, JULY 4, 1857.

O tenderly the haughty day
Fills his blue urn with fire;
One morn is in the mighty heaven,
And one in our desire.
The cannon booms from town to town,
Our pulses are not less,
The joy-bells chime their tidings down,
Which children's voices bless.
For He that flung the broad blue fold
O'er-mantling land and sea,
One third part of the sky unrolled
For the banner of the free.

The men are ripe of Saxon kind
To build an equal state,--
To take the statute from the mind,
And make of duty fate.
United States! the ages plead,--
Present and Past in under-song,--
Go put your creed into your deed,
Nor speak with double tongue.
For sea and land don't understand,
Nor skies without a frown
See rights for which the one hand fights
By the other cloven down.
Be just at home; then write your scroll
Of honour o'er the sea,
And bid the broad Atlantic roll,
A ferry of the free.
And, henceforth, there shall be no chain,
Save underneath the sea
The wires shall murmur through the main
Sweet songs of LIBERTY.
The conscious stars accord above,
The waters wild below,
And under, through the cable wove,
Her fiery errands go.
For He that worketh high and wise,
Nor pauses in his plan,
Will take the sun out of the skies
Ere freedom out of man.
BOSTON HYMN.
READ IN MUSIC HALL, JANUARY 1, 1863.
The word of the Lord by night
To the watching Pilgrims came,
As they sat by the seaside,

And filled their hearts with flame.
God said, I am tired of kings,
I suffer them no more;
Up to my ear the morning brings
The outrage of the poor.
Think ye I made this ball
A field of havoc and war,
Where tyrants great and tyrants small
Might harry the weak and poor?
My angel, his name is Freedom,--
Choose him to be your king;
He shall cut pathways east and west,
And fend you with his wing.
Lo! I uncover the land
Which I hid of old time in the West,
As the sculptor uncovers the statue
When he has wrought his best;
I show Columbia, of the rocks
Which dip their foot in the seas,
And soar to the air-borne flocks
Of clouds, and the boreal fleece.
I will divide my goods;
Call in the wretch and slave:
None shall rule but the humble,
And none but Toil shall have.
I will have never a noble,
No lineage counted great;
Fishers and choppers and ploughmen
Shall constitute a state.
Go, cut down trees in the forest,
And trim the straightest boughs;
Cut down the trees in the forest,
And build me a wooden house.

Call the people together,
The young men and the sires,
The digger in the harvest field,
Hireling, and him that hires;
And here in a pine state-house
They shall choose men to rule
In every needful faculty,
In church, and state, and school.
Lo, now! if these poor men
Can govern the land and sea,
And make just laws below the sun,
As planets faithful be.
And ye shall succour men;
'T is nobleness to serve;
Help them who cannot help again:
Beware from right to swerve.
I break your bonds and masterships,
And I unchain the slave:
Free be his heart and hand henceforth
As wind and wandering wave.
I cause from every creature
His proper good to flow:
As much as he is and doeth,
So much he shall bestow.
But laying hands on another
To coin his labour and sweat,
He goes in pawn to his victim
For eternal years in debt.
To-day unbind the captive,
So only are ye unbound;
Lift up a people from the dust,
Trump of their rescue, sound!
Pay ransom to the owner,

And fill the bag to the brim.
Who is the owner? The slave is owner,
And ever was. Pay him.
O North! give him beauty for rags,
And honour, O South! for his shame;
Nevada! coin thy golden crags
With Freedom's image and name.
Up! and the dusky race
That sat in darkness long,--
Be swift their feet as antelopes,
And as behemoth strong.
Come, East and West and North,
By races, as snow-flakes,
And carry my purpose forth,
Which neither halts nor shakes.
My will fulfilled shall be,
For, in daylight or in dark,
My thunderbolt has eyes to see
His way home to the mark.
VOLUNTARIES.
I.
Low and mournful be the strain,
Haughty thought be far from me;
Tones of penitence and pain,
Moanings of the tropic sea;
Low and tender in the cell
Where a captive sits in chains,
Crooning ditties treasured well
From his Afric's torrid plains.
Sole estate his sire bequeathed--
Hapless sire to hapless son--
Was the wailing song he breathed,
And his chain when life was done.

What his fault, or what his crime?
Or what ill planet crossed his prime?
Heart too soft and will too weak
To front the fate that crouches near,--
Dove beneath the vulture's beak;--
Will song dissuade the thirsty spear?
Dragged from his mother's arms and breast,
Displaced, disfurnished here,
His wistful toil to do his best
Chilled by a ribald jeer.
Great men in the Senate sate,
Sage and hero, side by side,
Building for their sons the State,
Which they shall rule with pride.
They forbore to break the chain
Which bound the dusky tribe,
Checked by the owners' fierce disdain,
Lured by "Union" as the bribe.
Destiny sat by, and said,
'Pang for pang your seed shall pay,
Hide in false peace your coward head,
I bring round the harvest-day.'
II.
Freedom all winged expands,
Nor perches in a narrow place;
Her broad van seeks unplanted lands;
She loves a poor and virtuous race.
Clinging to a colder zone
Whose dark sky sheds the snow-flake down,
The snow-flake is her banner's star,
Her stripes the boreal streamers are.
Long she loved the Northman well:
Now the iron age is done,

She will not refuse to dwell
With the offspring of the Sun;
Foundling of the desert far,
Where palms plume, siroccos blaze,
He roves unhurt the burning ways
In climates of the summer star.
He has avenues to God
Hid from men of Northern brain,
Far beholding, without cloud,
What these with slowest steps attain.
If once the generous chief arrive
To lead him willing to be led,
For freedom he will strike and strive,
And drain his heart till he be dead.
III.
In an age of fops and toys,
Wanting wisdom, void of right,
Who shall nerve heroic boys
To hazard all in Freedom's fight,--
Break sharply off their jolly games,
Forsake their comrades gay,
And quit proud homes and youthful dames,
For famine, toil, and fray?
Yet on the nimble air benign
Speed nimbler messages,
That waft the breath of grace divine
To hearts in sloth and ease.
So nigh is grandeur to our dust,
So near is God to man,
When Duty whispers low, Thou must,
The youth replies, I can.
IV.
O, well for the fortunate soul

Which Music's wings infold,
Stealing away the memory
Of sorrows new and old!
Yet happier he whose inward sight,
Stayed on his subtile thought,
Shuts his sense on toys of time,
To vacant bosoms brought.
But best befriended of the God
He who, in evil times,
Warned by an inward voice,
Heeds not the darkness and the dread,
Biding by his rule and choice,
Feeling only the fiery thread
Leading over heroic ground,
Walled with mortal terror round,
To the aim which him allures,
And the sweet heaven his deed secures.
Stainless soldier on the walls,
Knowing this,--and knows no more,--
Whoever fights, whoever falls,
Justice conquers evermore, Justice after as before,--
And he who battles on her side,
God, though he were ten times slain,
Crowns him victor glorified,
Victor over death and pain;
Forever: but his erring foe,
Self-assured that he prevails,
Looks from his victim lying low,
And sees aloft the red right arm
Redress the eternal scales.
He, the poor foe, whom angels foil,
Blind with pride, and fooled by hate,
Writhes within the dragon coil,

Reserved to a speechless fate.

V.

Blooms the laurel which belongs
To the valiant chief who fights;
I see the wreath, I hear the songs
Lauding the Eternal Rights,
Victors over daily wrongs:
Awful victors, they misguide
Whom they will destroy,
And their coming triumph hide
In our downfall, or our joy:
They reach no term, they never sleep,
In equal strength through space abide;
Though, feigning dwarfs, they crouch and creep,
The strong they slay, the swift outstride:
Fate's grass grows rank in valley clods,
And rankly on the castled steep,--
Speak it firmly, these are gods,
All are ghosts beside.

LOVE AND THOUGHT.

Two well-assorted travellers use
The highway, Eros and the Muse.
From the twins is nothing hidden,
To the pair is naught forbidden;
Hand in hand the comrades go
Every nook of nature through:
Each for other they were born,
Each can other best adorn;
They know one only mortal grief
Past all balsam or relief,
When, by false companions crossed,
The pilgrims have each other lost.

LOVER'S PETITION.

Good Heart, that ownest all!
I ask a modest boon and small:
Not of lands and towns the gift,--
Too large a load for me to lift,--
But for one proper creature,
Which geographic eye,
Sweeping the map of Western earth,
Or the Atlantic coast, from Maine
To Powhatan's domain,
Could not descry.
Is't much to ask in all thy huge creation,
So trivial a part,--
A solitary heart?
Yet count me not of spirit mean,
Or mine a mean demand,
For 't is the concentration
And worth of all the land,
The sister of the sea,
The daughter of the strand,
Composed of air and light,
And of the swart earth-might.
So little to thy poet's prayer
Thy large bounty well can spare.
And yet I think, if she were gone,
The world were better left alone.
UNA.
Roving, roving, as it seems,
Una lights my clouded dreams;
Still for journeys she is dressed;
We wander far by east and west.
In the homestead, homely thought;
At my work I ramble not;
If from home chance draw me wide,

Half-seen Una sits beside.
In my house and garden-plot,
Though beloved, I miss her not;
But one I seek in foreign places,
One face explore in foreign faces.
At home a deeper thought may light
The inward sky with chrysolite,
And I greet from far the ray,
Aurora of a dearer day.
But if upon the seas I sail,
Or trundle on the glowing rail,
I am but a thought of hers,
Loveliest of travellers.
So the gentle poet's name
To foreign parts is blown by fame;
Seek him in his native town,
He is hidden and unknown.
LETTERS.
Every day brings a ship,
Every ship brings a word;
Well for those who have no fear,
Looking seaward well assured
That the word the vessel brings
Is the word they wish to hear.
RUBIES.
They brought me rubies from the mine,
And held them to the sun;
I said, they are drops of frozen wine
From Eden's vats that run.
I looked again,--I thought them hearts
Of friends to friends unknown;
Tides that should warm each neighbouring life
Are locked in sparkling stone.

But fire to thaw that ruddy snow,
To break enchanted ice,
And give love's scarlet tides to flow,--
When shall that sun arise?
MERLIN'S SONG.
Of Merlin wise I learned a song,--
Sing it low or sing it loud,
It is mightier than the strong,
And punishes the proud.
I sing it to the surging crowd,--
Good men it will calm and cheer,
Bad men it will chain and cage.
In the heart of the music peals a strain
Which only angels hear;
Whether it waken joy or rage,
Hushed myriads hark in vain,
Yet they who hear it shed their age,
And take their youth again.
THE TEST. (Musa loquitur.)
I hung my verses in the wind,
Time and tide their faults may find.
All were winnowed through and through,
Five lines lasted sound and true;
Five were smelted in a pot.
Than the South more fierce and hot;
These the siroc could not melt,
Fire their fiercer flaming felt,
And the meaning was more white
Than July's meridian light.
Sunshine cannot bleach the snow,
Nor time unmake what poets know.
Have you eyes to find the five
Which five hundred did survive?

SOLUTION.

I am the Muse who sung alway
By Jove, at dawn of the first day.
Star-crowned, sole-sitting, long I wrought
To fire the stagnant earth with thought:
On spawning slime my song prevails,
Wolves shed their fangs, and dragons scales;
Flushed in the sky the sweet May-morn,
Earth smiled with flowers, and man was born.
Then Asia yeaned her shepherd race,
And Nile substructs her granite base,--
Tented Tartary, columned Nile,--
And, under vines, on rocky isle,
Or on wind-blown sea-marge bleak,
Forward stepped the perfect Greek:
That wit and joy might find a tongue,
And earth grow civil, HOMER Sung.
Flown to Italy from Greece,
I brooded long, and held my peace,
For I am wont to sing uncalled,
And in days of evil plight
Unlock doors of new delight;
And sometimes mankind I appalled
With a bitter horoscope,
With spasms of terror for balm of hope.
Then by better thought I lead
Bards to speak what nations need;
So I folded me in fears,
And DANTE searched the triple spheres,
Moulding nature at his will,
So shaped, so coloured, swift or still,
And, sculptor-like, his large design
Etched on Alp and Apennine.

Seethed in mists of Penmanmaur,
Taught by Plinlimmon's Druid power,
England's genius filled all measure
Of heart and soul, of strength and pleasure,
Gave to the mind its emperor,
And life was larger than before:
Nor sequent centuries could hit
Orbit and sum of SHAKSPEARE's wit.
The men who lived with him became
Poets, for the air was fame.
Far in the North, where polar night
Holds in check the frolic light,
In trance upborne past mortal goal
The Swede EMANUEL leads the soul.
Through snows above, mines underground,
The inks of Erebus he found;
Rehearsed to men the damned wails
On which the seraph music sails,
In spirit-worlds he trod alone,
But walked the earth unmarked, unknown.
The near by-stander caught no sound,--
Yet they who listened far aloof
Heard rendings of the skyey roof,
And felt, beneath, the quaking ground;
And his air-sown, unheeded words,
In the next age, are flaming swords.
In newer days of war and trade,
Romance forgot, and faith decayed,
When Science armed and guided war,
And clerks the Janus-gates unbar,
When France, where poet never grew,
Halved and dealt the globe anew,
GOETHE, raised o'er joy and strife,

Drew the firm lines of Fate and Life,
And brought Olympian wisdom down
To court and mart, to gown and town,
Stooping, his finger wrote in clay
The open secret of to-day.
So bloom the unfading petals five,
And verses that all verse outlive.

NATURE AND LIFE.

NATURE.

I.

Winters know
Easily to shed the snow,
And the untaught Spring is wise
In cowslips and anemonies.
Nature, hating art and pains,
Baulks and baffles plotting brains;
Casualty and Surprise
Are the apples of her eyes;
But she dearly loves the poor,
And, by marvel of her own,
Strikes the loud pretender down.
For Nature listens in the rose,
And hearkens in the berry's bell,
To help her friends, to plague her foes,
And like wise God she judges well.
Yet doth much her love excel
To the souls that never fell,
To swains that live in happiness,
And do well because they please,
Who walk in ways that are unfamed,

And feats achieve before they're named.
NATURE.
II.
She is gamesome and good,
But of mutable mood,--
No dreary repeater now and again,
She will be all things to all men.
She who is old, but nowise feeble,
Pours her power into the people,
Merry and manifold without bar,
Makes and moulds them what they are,
And what they call their city way
Is not their way, but hers,
And what they say they made to-day,
They learned of the oaks and firs.
She spawneth men as mallows fresh,
Hero and maiden, flesh of her flesh;
She drugs her water and her wheat
With the flavours she finds meet,
And gives them what to drink and eat;
And having thus their bread and growth,
They do her bidding, nothing loath.
What's most theirs is not their own,
But borrowed in atoms from iron and stone,
And in their vaunted works of Art
The master-stroke is still her part.
THE ROMANY GIRL.
The sun goes down, and with him takes
The coarseness of my poor attire;
The fair moon mounts, and aye the flame
Of Gypsy beauty blazes higher.
Pale Northern girls! you scorn our race;
You captives of your air-tight halls,

Wear out in-doors your sickly days,
But leave us the horizon walls.
And if I take you, dames, to task,
And say it frankly without guile,
Then you are Gypsies in a mask,
And I the lady all the while.
If, on the heath, below the moon,
I court and play with paler blood,
Me false to mine dare whisper none,--
One sallow horseman knows me good.
Go, keep your cheek's rose from the rain,
For teeth and hair with shopmen deal;
My swarthy tint is in the grain,
The rocks and forest know it real.
The wild air bloweth in our lungs,
The keen stars twinkle in our eyes,
The birds gave us our wily tongues,
The panther in our dances flies.
You doubt we read the stars on high,
Nathless we read your fortunes true;
The stars may hide in the upper sky,
But without glass we fathom you.
DAYS.
Damsels of Time, the hypocritic Days,
Muffled and dumb like barefoot dervishes,
And marching single in an endless file,
Bring diadems and fagots in their hands.
To each they offer gifts after his will,
Bread, kingdoms, stars, and sky that holds them all.
I, in my pleached garden, watched the pomp,
Forgot my morning wishes, hastily
Took a few herbs and apples, and the Day
Turned and departed silent. I, too late,

Under her solemn fillet saw the scorn.

THE CHARTIST'S COMPLAINT.

Day! hast thou two faces,
Making one place two places?
One, by humble farmer seen,
Chill and wet, unlighted, mean,
Useful only, triste and damp,
Serving for a labourer's lamp?
Have the same mists another side,
To be the appanage of pride,
Gracing the rich man's wood and lake,
His park where amber mornings break,
And treacherously bright to show
His planted isle where roses glow?
O Day! and is your mightiness
A sycophant to smug success?
Will the sweet sky and ocean broad
Be fine accomplices to fraud?
O Sun! I curse thy cruel ray:
Back, back to chaos, harlot Day!

MY GARDEN.

If I could put my woods in song,
And tell what's there enjoyed,
All men would to my gardens throng,
And leave the cities void.

In my plot no tulips blow,--
Snow-loving pines and oaks instead;
And rank the savage maples grow
From spring's faint flush to autumn red.

My garden is a forest ledge
Which older forests bound;
The banks slope down to the blue lake-edge,
Then plunge to depths profound.

Here once the Deluge ploughed,
Laid the terraces, one by one;
Ebbing later whence it flowed,
They bleach and dry in the sun.
The sowers made haste to depart,--
The wind and the birds which sowed it;
Not for fame, nor by rules of art,
Planted these, and tempests flowed it.
Waters that wash my garden side
Play not in Nature's lawful web,
They heed not moon or solar tide,--
Five years elapse from flood to ebb.
Hither hasted, in old time, Jove,
And every god,--none did refuse;
And be sure at last came Love,
And after Love, the Muse.
Keen ears can catch a syllable,
As if one spake to another,
In the hemlocks tall, untameable,
And what the whispering grasses smother.
AEolian harps in the pine
Ring with the song of the Fates;
Infant Bacchus in the vine,--
Far distant yet his chorus waits.
Cast thou copy in verse one chime
Of the wood-bell's peal and cry,
Write in a book the morning's prime,
Or match with words that tender sky?
Wonderful verse of the gods,
Of one import, of varied tone;
They chant the bliss of their abodes
To man imprisoned in his own.
Ever the words of the gods resound;

But the porches of man's ear
Seldom in this low life's round
Are unsealed, that he may hear.
Wandering voices in the air,
And murmurs in the wold,
Speak what I cannot declare,
Yet cannot all withhold.
When the shadow fell on the lake,
The whirlwind in ripples wrote
Air-bells of fortune that shine and break,
And omens above thought.
But the meanings cleave to the lake,
Cannot be carried in book or urn;
Go thy ways now, come later back,
On waves and hedges still they burn.
These the fates of men forecast,
Of better men than live to-day;
If who can read them comes at last,
He will spell in the sculpture, 'Stay!'

THE TITMOUSE.

You shall not be overbold
When you deal with arctic cold,
As late I found my lukewarm blood
Chilled wading in the snow-choked wood.
How should I fight? my foeman fine
Has million arms to one of mine:
East, west, for aid I looked in vain,
East, west, north, south, are his domain.
Miles off, three dangerous miles, is home;
Must borrow his winds who there would come.
Up and away for life! be fleet!--
The frost-king ties my fumbling feet,
Sings in my ears, my hands are stones,

Curdles the blood to the marble bones,
Tugs at the heart-strings, numbs the sense,
And hems in life with narrowing fence.
Well, in this broad bed lie and sleep,
The punctual stars will vigil keep,
Embalmed by purifying cold,
The winds shall sing their dead-march old,
The snow is no ignoble shroud,
The moon thy mourner, and the cloud.
Softly,--but this way fate was pointing,
'T was coming fast to such anointing,
When piped a tiny voice hard by,
Gay and polite a cheerful cry,
Chic-chicadeedee! saucy note
Out of sound heart and merry throat,
As if it said, 'Good day, good sir!
Fine afternoon, old passenger!
Happy to meet you in these places,
Where January brings few faces.'
This poet, though he live apart,
Moved by his hospitable heart,
Sped, when I passed his sylvan fort,
To do the honours of his court,
As fits a feathered lord of land;
Flew near, with soft wing grazed my hand,
Hopped on the bough, then, darting low,
Prints his small impress on the snow,
Shows feats of his gymnastic play,
Head downward, clinging to the spray.
Here was this atom in full breath,
Hurling defiance at vast death;
This scrap of valour just for play
Fronts the north-wind in waistcoat gray,

As if to shame my weak behaviour;
I greeted loud my little saviour,
'You pet! what dost here? and what for?
In these woods, thy small Labrador,
At this pinch, wee San Salvador!
What fire burns in that little chest
So frolic, stout, and self-possest?
Henceforth I wear no stripe but thine;
Ashes and jet all hues outshine.
Why are not diamonds black and gray,
To ape thy dare-devil array?
And I affirm, the spacious North
Exists to draw thy virtue forth.
I think no virtue goes with size;
The reason of all cowardice
Is, that men are overgrown,
And, to be valiant, must come down
To the titmouse dimension.'
'T is good-will makes intelligence,
And I began to catch the sense
Of my bird's song: 'Live out of doors,
In the great woods, on prairie floors.
I dine in the sun; when he sinks in the sea,
I too have a hole in a hollow tree;
And I like less when Summer beats
With stifling beams on these retreats,
Than noontide twilights which snow makes
With tempest of the blinding flakes.
For well the soul, if stout within,
Can arm impregnably the skin;
And polar frost my frame defied,
Made of the air that blows outside.'
With glad remembrance of my debt,

I homeward turn; farewell, my pet!
When here again thy pilgrim comes,
He shall bring store of seeds and crumbs.
Doubt not, so long as earth has bread,
Thou first and foremost shalt be fed;
The Providence that is most large
Takes hearts like thine in special charge,
Helps who for their own need are strong,
And the sky dotes on cheerful song.
Henceforth I prize thy wiry chant
O'er all that mass and minster vaunt;
For men mis-hear thy call in spring,
As 't would accost some frivolous wing;
Crying out of the hazel copse, Phe-be!
And, in winter, Chic-a-dee-dee!
I think old Caesar must have heard
In northern Gaul my dauntless bird,
And, echoed in some frosty wold,
Borrowed thy battle-numbers bold.
And I will write our annals new,
And thank thee for a better clew,
I, who dreamed not when I came here
To find the antidote of fear,
Now hear thee say in Roman key,
Paean! Veni, vidi, vici.
SEA-SHORE.
I heard or seemed to hear the chiding Sea
Say, Pilgrim, why so late and slow to come?
Am I not always here, thy summer home?
Is not my voice thy music, morn and eve?
My breath thy healthful climate in the heats,
My touch thy antidote, my bay thy bath?
Was ever building like my terraces?

Was ever couch magnificent as mine?
Lie on the warm rock-ledges, and there learn
A little hut suffices like a town.
I make your sculptured architecture vain,
Vain beside mine. I drive my wedges home,
And carve the coastwise mountain into caves.
Lo! here is Rome, and Nineveh, and Thebes,
Karnak, and Pyramid, and Giant's Stairs,
Half piled or prostrate; and my newest slab
Older than all thy race.
Behold the Sea,
The opaline, the plentiful and strong,
Yet beautiful as is the rose in June,
Fresh as the trickling rainbow of July;
Sea full of food, the nourisher of kinds,
Purger of earth, and medicine of men;
Creating a sweet climate by my breath,
Washing out harms and griefs from memory,
And, in my mathematic ebb and flow,
Giving a hint of that which changes not.
Rich are the sea-gods:--who gives gifts but they?
They grope the sea for pearls, but more than pearls:
They pluck Force thence, and give it to the wise.
For every wave is wealth to Daedalus,
Wealth to the cunning artist who can work
This matchless strength. Where shall he find, O waves!
A load your Atlas shoulders cannot lift?
I with my hammer pounding evermore
The rocky coast, smite Andes into dust,
Strewing my bed, and, in another age,
Rebuild a continent of better men.
Then I unbar the doors: my paths lead out
The exodus of nations: I disperse

Men to all shores that front the hoary main.
I too have arts and sorceries;
Illusion dwells forever with the wave.
I know what spells are laid. Leave me to deal
With credulous and imaginative man;
For, though he scoop my water in his palm,
A few rods off he deems it gems and clouds.
Planting strange fruits and sunshine on the shore,
I make some coast alluring, some lone isle,
To distant men, who must go there, or die.

SONG OF NATURE.

Mine are the night and morning,
The pits of air, the gulf of space,
The sportive sun, the gibbous moon,
The innumerable days.
I hide in the solar glory,
I am dumb in the pealing song,
I rest on the pitch of the torrent,
In slumber I am strong.
No numbers have counted my tallies,
No tribes my house can fill,
I sit by the shining Fount of Life,
And pour the deluge still;
And ever by delicate powers
Gathering along the centuries
From race on race the rarest flowers,
My wreath shall nothing miss.
And many a thousand summers
My apples ripened well,
And light from meliorating stars
With firmer glory fell.
I wrote the past in characters
Of rock and fire the scroll,

The building in the coral sea,
The planting of the coal.
And thefts from satellites and rings
And broken stars I drew,
And out of spent and aged things
I formed the world anew;
What time the gods kept carnival,
Tricked out in star and flower,
And in cramp elf and saurian forms
They swathed their too much power.
Time and thought were my surveyors,
They laid their courses well,
They boiled the sea, and baked the layers
Of granite, marl, and shell.
But he, the man-child glorious,--
Where tarries he the while?
The rainbow shines his harbinger,
The sunset gleams his smile.
My boreal lights leap upward,
Forthright my planets roll,
And still the man-child is not born,
The summit of the whole.
Must time and tide for ever run?
Will never my winds go sleep in the west?
Will never my wheels which whirl the sun
And satellites have rest?
Too much of donning and doffing,
Too slow the rainbow fades,
I weary of my robe of snow,
My leaves and my cascades;
I tire of globes and races,
Too long the game is played;
What without him is summer's pomp,

Or winter's frozen shade?
I travail in pain for him,
My creatures travail and wait;
His couriers come by squadrons,
He comes not to the gate.
Twice I have moulded an image,
And thrice outstretched my hand,
Made one of day, and one of night,
And one of the salt sea-sand.
One in a Judaean manger,
And one by Avon stream,
One over against the mouths of Nile,
And one in the Academe.
I moulded kings and saviours,
And bards o'er kings to rule;--
But fell the starry influence short,
The cup was never full.
Yet whirl the glowing wheels once more,
And mix the bowl again;
Seethe, Fate! the ancient elements,
Heat, cold, wet, dry, and peace, and pain.
Let war and trade and creeds and song
Blend, ripen race on race,
The sunburnt world a man shall breed
Of all the zones, and countless days.
No ray is dimmed, no atom worn,
My oldest force is good as new,
And the fresh rose on yonder thorn
Gives back the bending heavens in dew.
TWO RIVERS.
Thy summer voice, Musketaquit,
Repeats the music of the rain;
But sweeter rivers pulsing flit

Through thee, as thou through Concord Plain.
Thou in thy narrow banks are pent:
The stream I love unbounded goes
Through flood and sea and firmament;
Through light, through life, it forward flows.
I see the inundation sweet,
I hear the spending of the stream
Through years, through men, through nature fleet,
Through passion, thought, through power and dream.
Musketaquit, a goblin strong,
Of shard and flint makes jewels gay;
They lose their grief who hear his song,
And where he winds is the day of day.
So forth and brighter fares my stream,--
Who drinks it shall not thirst again;
No darkness stains its equal gleam,
And ages drop in it like rain.

WALDEINSAMKEIT.

I do not count the hours I spend
In wandering by the sea;
The forest is my loyal friend,
Like God it useth me.
In plains that room for shadows make
Of skirting hills to lie,
Bound in by streams which give and take
Their colours from the sky;
Or on the mountain-crest sublime,
Or down the oaken glade,
O what have I to do with time?
For this the day was made.
Cities of mortals woe begone
Fantastic care derides,
But in the serious landscape lone

Stern benefit abides.
Sheen will tarnish, honey cloy,
And merry is only a mask of sad,
But, sober on a fund of joy,
The woods at heart are glad.
There the great Planter plants
Of fruitful worlds the grain,
And with a million spells enchants
The souls that walk in pain.
Still on the seeds of all he made
The rose of beauty burns;
Through times that wear, and forms that fade,
Immortal youth returns.
The black ducks mounting from the lake,
The pigeon in the pines,
The bittern's boom, a desert make
Which no false art refines.
Down in yon watery nook,
Where bearded mists divide,
The gray old gods whom Chaos knew,
The sires of Nature, hide.
Aloft, in secret veins of air,
Blows the sweet breath of song,
O, few to scale those uplands dare,
Though they to all belong!
See thou bring not to field or stone
The fancies found in books;
Leave authors' eyes, and fetch your own,
To brave the landscape's looks.
And if, amid this dear delight,
My thoughts did home rebound,
I well might reckon it a slight
To the high cheer I found.

Oblivion here thy wisdom is,
Thy thrift, the sleep of cares;
For a proud idleness like this
Crowns all thy mean affairs.
TERMINUS.
It is time to be old,
To take in sail:--
The god of bounds,
Who sets to seas a shore,
Came to me in his fatal rounds,
And said: 'No more!
No farther spread
Thy broad ambitious branches, and thy root.
Fancy departs: no more invent,
Contract thy firmament
To compass of a tent.
There's not enough for this and that,
Make thy option which of two;
Economize the failing river,
Not the less revere the Giver,
Leave the many and hold the few.
Timely wise accept the terms,
Soften the fall with wary foot;
A little while
Still plan and smile,
And, fault of novel germs,
Mature the unfallen fruit.
Curse, if thou wilt, thy sires,
Bad husbands of their fires,
Who, when they gave thee breath,
Failed to bequeath
The needful sinew stark as once,
The Baresark marrow to thy bones,

But left a legacy of ebbing veins,
Inconstant heat and nerveless reins,--
Amid the Muses, left thee deaf and dumb,
Amid the gladiators, halt and numb.'
As the bird trims her to the gale,
I trim myself to the storm of time,
I man the rudder, reef the sail,
Obey the voice at eve obeyed at prime:
'Lowly faithful, banish fear,
Right onward drive unarmed;
The port, well worth the cruise, is near,
And every wave is charmed.'
THE PAST.
The debt is paid,
The verdict said,
The Furies laid,
The plague is stayed,
All fortunes made;
Turn the key and bolt the door,
Sweet is death forevermore.
Nor haughty hope, nor swart chagrin,
Nor murdering hate, can enter in.
All is now secure and fast;
Not the gods can shake the Past;
Flies to the adamantine door
Bolted down forevermore.
None can re-enter there,
No thief so politic,
No Satan with a royal trick
Steal in by window, chink, or hole,
To bind or unbind, add what lacked,
Insert a leaf, or forge a name,
New-face or finish what is packed,

Alter or mend eternal Fact.

THE LAST FAREWELL.

LINES WRITTEN BY THE AUTHOR'S BROTHER, EDWARD BLISS EMERSON, WHILST SAILING OUT OF BOSTON HAR- BOUR, BOUND FOR THE ISLAND OF PORTO RICO, IN 1832.

Farewell, ye lofty spires
That cheered the holy light!
Farewell, domestic fires
That broke the gloom of night!
Too soon those spires are lost,
Too fast we leave the bay,
Too soon by ocean tost
From hearth and home away,
Far away, far away.
Farewell the busy town,
The wealthy and the wise,
Kind smile and honest frown
From bright, familiar eyes.
All these are fading now;
Our brig hastes on her way,
Her unremembering prow
Is leaping o'er the sea,
Far away, far away.
Farewell, my mother fond,
Too kind, too good to me;
Nor pearl nor diamond
Would pay my debt to thee.
But even thy kiss denies
Upon my cheek to stay;
The winged vessel flies,
And billows round her play,
Far away, far away.
Farewell, my brothers true,

My betters, yet my peers;
How desert without you
My few and evil years!
But though aye one in heart,
Together sad or gay,
Rude ocean doth us part;
We separate to-day,
Far away, far away.
Farewell I breathe again
To dim New England's shore;
My heart shall beat not when
I pant for thee no more.
In yon green palmy isle,
Beneath the tropic ray,
I murmur never while
For thee and thine I pray;
Far away, far away.

IN MEMORIAM.

E. B. E.

I mourn upon this battle-field,
But not for those who perished here.
Behold the river-bank
Whither the angry farmers came,
In sloven dress and broken rank,
Nor thought of fame.
Their deed of blood
All mankind praise;
Even the serene Reason says,
It was well done.
The wise and simple have one glance
To greet yon stern head-stone,
Which more of pride than pity gave
To mark the Briton's friendless grave.

Yet it is a stately tomb;
The grand return
Of eve and morn,
The year's fresh bloom,
The silver cloud,
Might grace the dust that is most proud.
Yet not of these I muse
In this ancestral place,
But of a kindred face
That never joy or hope shall here diffuse.
Ah, brother of the brief but blazing star!
What hast thou to do with these
Haunting this bank's historic trees?
Thou born for noblest life,
For action's field, for victor's car,
Thou living champion of the right?
To these their penalty belonged:
I grudge not these their bed of death,
But thine to thee, who never wronged
The poorest that drew breath.
All inborn power that could
Consist with homage to the good
Flamed from his martial eye;
He who seemed a soldier born,
He should have the helmet worn,
All friends to fend, all foes defy,
Fronting foes of God and man,
Frowning down the evil-doer,
Battling for the weak and poor.
His from youth the leader's look
Gave the law which others took,
And never poor beseeching glance
Shamed that sculptured countenance.

There is no record left on earth,
Save in tablets of the heart,
Of the rich inherent worth,
Of the grace that on him shone,
Of eloquent lips, of joyful wit;
He could not frame a word unfit,
An act unworthy to be done;
Honour prompted every glance,
Honour came and sat beside him,
In lowly cot or painful road,
And evermore the cruel god
Cried, "Onward!" and the palm-crown showed.
Born for success he seemed,
With grace to win, with heart to hold,
With shining gifts that took all eyes,
With budding power in college-halls,
As pledged in coming days to forge
Weapons to guard the State, or scourge
Tyrants despite their guards or walls.
On his young promise Beauty smiled,
Drew his free homage unbeguiled,
And prosperous Age held out his hand,
And richly his large future planned,
And troops of friends enjoyed the tide,--
All, all was given, and only health denied.
I see him with superior smile
Hunted by Sorrow's grisly train
In lands remote, in toil and pain,
With angel patience labour on,
With the high port he wore erewhile,
When, foremost of the youthful band,
The prizes in all lists he won;
Nor bate one jot of heart or hope,

And, least of all, the loyal tie
Which holds to home 'neath every sky,
The joy and pride the pilgrim feels
In hearts which round the hearth at home
Keep pulse for pulse with those who roam.
What generous beliefs console
The brave whom Fate denies the goal!
If others reach it, is content;
To Heaven's high will his will is bent.
Firm on his heart relied,
What lot soe'er betide,
Work of his hand
He nor repents nor grieves,
Pleads for itself the fact,
As unrepenting Nature leaves
Her every act.
Fell the bolt on the branching oak;
The rainbow of his hope was broke;
No craven cry, no secret tear,--
He told no pang, he knew no fear;
Its peace sublime his aspect kept,
His purpose woke, his features slept;
And yet between the spasms of pain
His genius beamed with joy again.
O'er thy rich dust the endless smile
Of Nature in thy Spanish isle
Hints never loss or cruel break
And sacrifice for love's dear sake,
Nor mourn the unalterable Days
That Genius goes and Folly stays.
What matters how, or from what ground,
The freed soul its Creator found?
Alike thy memory embalms

That orange-grove, that isle of palms,
And these loved banks, whose oak-boughs bold
Root in the blood of heroes old.

ELEMENTS.

EXPERIENCE.
The lords of life, the lords of life,--
I saw them pass,
In their own guise,
Like and unlike,
Portly and grim,--
Use and Surprise,
Surface and Dream,
Succession swift and spectral Wrong,
Temperament without a tongue,
And the inventor of the game
Omnipresent without name;--
Some to see, some to be guessed,
They march from east to west:
Little man, least of all,
Among the legs of his guardians tall,
Walked about with puzzled look.
Him by the hand dear Nature took,
Dearest Nature, strong and kind,
Whispered, 'Darling, never mind!
To-morrow they will wear another face,
The founder thou; these are thy race!'
COMPENSATION.
II.
The wings of Time are black and white,
Pied with morning and with night.
Mountain tall and ocean deep

Trembling balance duly keep.
In changing moon and tidal wave
Glows the feud of Want and Have.
Gauge of more and less through space,
Electric star or pencil plays,
The lonely Earth amid the balls
That hurry through the eternal halls,
A makeweight flying to the void,
Supplemental asteroid,
Or compensatory spark,
Shoots across the neutral Dark.

III.

Man's the elm, and Wealth the vine;
Staunch and strong the tendrils twine:
Though the frail ringlets thee deceive,
None from its stock that vine can reave.
Fear not, then, thou child infirm,
There's no god dare wrong a worm;
Laurel crowns cleave to deserts,
And power to him who power exerts.
Hast not thy share? On winged feet,
Lo! it rushes thee to meet;
And all that Nature made thy own,
Floating in air or pent in stone,
Will rive the hills and swim the sea,
And, like thy shadow, follow thee.

POLITICS.

Gold and iron are good
To buy iron and gold;
All earth's fleece and food
For their like are sold.
Hinted Merlin wise,
Proved Napoleon great,

Nor kind nor coinage buys
Aught above its rate.
Fear, Craft, and Avarice
Cannot rear a State.
Out of dust to build
What is more than dust,--
Walls Amphion piled
Phoebus stablish must.
When the Muses nine
When the Virtues meet,
Find to their design
An Atlantic seat,
By green orchard boughs
Fended from the heat,
Where the statesman ploughs
Furrow for the wheat,--
When the Church is social worth,
When the state-house is the hearth,
Then the perfect State is come,
The republican at home.
HEROISM.
Ruby wine is drunk by knaves,
Sugar spends to fatten slaves,
Rose and vine-leaf deck buffoons;
Thunder-clouds are Jove's festoons,
Drooping oft in wreaths of dread,
Lightning-knotted round his head;
The hero is not fed on sweets,
Daily his own heart he eats;
Chambers of the great are jails,
And head-winds right for royal sails.
CHARACTER.
The sun set, but set not his hope:

Stars rose; his faith was earlier up:
Fixed on the enormous galaxy,
Deeper and older seemed his eye;
And matched his sufferance sublime
The taciturnity of time.
He spoke, and words more soft than rain
Brought the Age of Gold again:
His action won such reverence sweet
As hid all measure of the feat.
CULTURE.
Can rules or tutors educate
The semigod whom we await?
He must be musical,
Tremulous, impressional,
Alive to gentle influence
Of landscape and of sky,
And tender to the spirit-touch
Of man's or maiden's eye:
But, to his native centre fast,
Shall into Future fuse the Past,
And the world's flowing fates in his own mould recast.
FRIENDSHIP.
A ruddy drop of manly blood
The surging sea outweighs,
The world uncertain comes and goes,
The lover rooted stays.
I fancied he was fled,--
And, after many a year,
Glowed unexhausted kindliness,
Like daily sunrise there.
My careful heart was free again,
O friend, my bosom said,
Through thee alone the sky is arched,

Through thee the rose is red;
All things through thee take nobler form,
And look beyond the earth,
The mill-round of our fate appears
A sun-path in thy worth.
Me too thy nobleness has taught
To master my despair;
The fountains of my hidden life
Are through thy friendship fair.
BEAUTY.
Was never form and never face
So sweet to SEYD as only grace
Which did not slumber like a stone,
But hovered gleaming and was gone.
Beauty chased he everywhere,
In flame, in storm, in clouds of air.
He smote the lake to feed his eye
With the beryl beam of the broken wave;
He flung in pebbles well to hear
The moment's music which they gave.
Oft pealed for him a lofty tone
From nodding pole and belting zone.
He heard a voice none else could hear
From centred and from errant sphere.
The quaking earth did quake in rhyme,
Seas ebbed and flowed in epic chime.
In dens of passion, and pits of woe,
He saw strong Eros struggling through,
To sun the dark and solve the curse,
And beam to the bounds of the universe.
While thus to love he gave his days
In loyal worship, scorning praise,
How spread their lures for him in vain

Thieving Ambition and paltering Gain!
He thought it happier to be dead,
To die for Beauty, than live for bread.
MANNERS.
Grace, Beauty, and Caprice
Build this golden portal;
Graceful women, chosen men,
Dazzle every mortal.
Their sweet and lofty countenance
His enchanted food;
He need not go to them, their forms
Beset his solitude.
He looketh seldom in their face,
His eyes explore the ground,--
The green grass is a looking-glass
Whereon their traits are found.
Little and less he says to them,
So dances his heart in his breast;
Their tranquil mien bereaveth him
Of wit, of words, of rest.
Too weak to win, too fond to shun
The tyrants of his doom,
The much deceived Endymion
Slips behind a tomb.
ART.
Give to barrows, trays, and pans
Grace and glimmer of romance;
Bring the moonlight into noon
Hid in gleaming piles of stone;
On the city's paved street
Plant gardens lined with lilacs sweet;
Let spouting fountains cool the air,
Singing in the sun-baked square;

Let statue, picture, park, and hall,
Ballad, flag, and festival,
The past restore, the day adorn,
And make to-morrow a new morn.
So shall the drudge in dusty frock
Spy behind the city clock
Retinues of airy kings,
Skirts of angels, starry wings,
His fathers shining in bright fables,
His children fed at heavenly tables.
'T is the privilege of Art
Thus to play its cheerful part,
Man on earth to acclimate,
And bend the exile to his fate,
And, moulded of one element
With the days and firmament,
Teach him on these as stairs to climb,
And live on even terms with Time;
Whilst upper life the slender rill
Of human sense doth overfill.

SPIRITUAL LAWS.

The living Heaven thy prayers respect,
House at once and architect,
Quarrying man's rejected hours,
Builds therewith eternal towers;
Sole and self-commanded works,
Fears not undermining days,
Grows by decays,
And, by the famous might that lurks
In reaction and recoil,
Makes flame to freeze and ice to boil;
Forging, through swart arms of Offence,
The silver seat of Innocence.

UNITY.

Space is ample, east and west,
But two cannot go abreast,
Cannot travel in it two:
Yonder masterful cuckoo
Crowds every egg out of the nest,
Quick or dead, except its own;
A spell is laid on sod and stone,
Night and day were tampered with,
Every quality and pith
Surcharged and sultry with a power
That works its will on age and hour.

WORSHIP.

This is he, who, felled by foes,
Sprung harmless up, refreshed by blows:
He to captivity was sold,
But him no prison-bars would hold:
Though they sealed him in a rock,
Mountain chains he can unlock:
Thrown to lions for their meat,
The crouching lion kissed his feet:
Bound to the stake, no flames appalled,
But arched o'er him an honouring vault.
This is he men miscall Fate,
Threading dark ways, arriving late,
But ever coming in time to crown
The truth, and hurl wrong-doers down.
He is the oldest, and best known,
More near than aught thou call'st thy own,
Yet, greeted in another's eyes,
Disconcerts with glad surprise.
This is Jove, who, deaf to prayers,
Floods with blessings unawares.

Draw, if thou canst, the mystic line
Severing rightly his from thine,
Which is human, which divine.

QUATRAINS.

S. H.
With beams December planets dart
His cold eye truth and conduct scanned,
July was in his sunny heart,
October in his liberal hand.
H.
High was her heart, and yet was well inclined,
Her manners made of bounty well refined;
Far capitals, and marble courts, her eye still seemed to see,
Minstrels, and kings, and high-born dames, and of the best that be.
"SUUM CUIQUE."
Wilt thou seal up the avenues of ill?
Pay every debt, as if God wrote the bill.
HUSH!
Every thought is public,
Every nook is wide;
Thy gossips spread each whisper,
And the gods from side to side.
ORATOR.
He who has no hands
Perforce must use his tongue;
Foxes are so cunning
Because they are not strong.
ARTIST.
Quit the hut, frequent the palace,
Reck not what the people say;

For still, where'er the trees grow biggest,
Huntsmen find the easiest way.
POET.
Ever the Poet from the land
Steers his bark, and trims his sail;
Right out to sea his courses stand,
New worlds to find in pinnace frail.
POET.
To clothe the fiery thought
In simple words succeeds,
For still the craft of genius is
To mask a king in weeds.
BOTANIST.
Go thou to thy learned task,
I stay with the flowers of spring:
Do thou of the ages ask
What me the flowers will bring.
GARDENER.
True Bramin, in the morning meadows wet,
Expound the Vedas of the violet,
Or, hid in vines, peeping through many a loop,
See the plum redden, and the beurre stoop.
FORESTER.
He took the colour of his vest
From rabbit's coat or grouse's breast;
For, as the wood-kinds lurk and hide,
So walks the woodman, unespied.
NORTHMAN.
The gale that wrecked you on the sand,
It helped my rowers to row;
The storm is my best galley hand,
And drives me where I go.
FROM ALCUIN.

The sea is the road of the bold,
Frontier of the wheat-sown plains,
The pit wherein the streams are rolled,
And fountain of the rains.
EXCELSIOR.
Over his head were the maple buds,
And over the tree was the moon,
And over the moon were the starry studs,
That drop from the angel's shoon.
BORROWING.
FROM THE FRENCH.
Some of your hurts you have cured,
And the sharpest you still have survived,
But what torments of grief you endured
From evils which never arrived!
NATURE.
Boon Nature yields each day a brag which we now first behold, And trains us on to slight the new, as if it were the old:
But blest is he, who, playing deep, yet haply asks not why, Too busied with the crowded hour to fear to live or die.
FATE.
Her planted eye to-day controls,
Is in the morrow most at home,
And sternly calls to being souls
That curse her when they come.
HOROSCOPE.
Ere he was born, the stars of fate
Plotted to make him rich and great:
When from the womb the babe was loosed,
The gate of gifts behind him closed.
POWER.
Cast the bantling on the rocks,
Suckle him with the she-wolf's teat,

Wintered with the hawk and fox,
Power and speed be hands and feet.
CLIMACTERIC.
I am not wiser for my age,
Nor skilful by my grief;
Life loiters at the book's first page,--
Ah! could we turn the leaf.
HERI, CRAS, HODIE.
Shines the last age, the next with hope is seen,
To-day slinks poorly off unmarked between:
Future or Past no richer secret folds,
O friendless Present! than thy bosom holds.
MEMORY.
Night-dreams trace on Memory's wall
Shadows of the thoughts of day,
And thy fortunes, as they fall,
The bias of the will betray.
LOVE.
Love on his errand bound to go
Can swim the flood, and wade through snow,
Where way is none, 'twill creep and wind
And eat through Alps its home to find.
SACRIFICE.
Though love repine, and reason chafe,
There came a voice without reply,--
"Tis man's perdition to be safe,
When for the truth he ought to die.'
PERICLES.
Well and wisely said the Greek,
Be thou faithful, but not fond;
To the altar's foot thy fellow seek,
The Furies wait beyond.
CASELLA.

Test of the poet is knowledge of love,
For Eros is older than Saturn or Jove;
Never was poet, of late or of yore,
Who was not tremulous with love-lore.
SHAKSPEARE.
I see all human wits
Are measured but a few,
Unmeasured still my Shakspeare sits,
Lone as the blessed Jew.
HAFIZ.
Her passions the shy violet
From Hafiz never hides;
Love-longings of the raptured bird
The bird to him confides.
NATURE IN LEASTS.
As sings the pine-tree in the wind,
So sings in the wind a sprig of the pine;
Her strength and soul has laughing France
Shed in each drop of wine.
[GREEK TITLE].
'A new commandment,' said the smiling Muse,
'I give my darling son, Thou shalt not preach;'--
Luther, Fox, Behmen, Swedenborg, grew pale,
And, on the instant, rosier clouds upbore
Hafiz and Shakspeare with their shining choirs.

TRANSLATIONS.

SONNET OF MICHEL ANGELO BUONAROTI.
Never did sculptor's dream unfold
A form which marble doth not hold
In its white block; yet it therein shall find
Only the hand secure and bold

Which still obeys the mind.
So hide in thee, thou heavenly dame,
The ill I shun, the good I claim;
I, alas! not well alive,
Miss the aim whereto I strive.
Not love, nor beauty's pride,
Not fortune, nor thy coldness, can I chide,
If, whilst within thy heart abide
Both death and pity, my unequal skill
Fails of the life, but draws the death and ill.
THE EXILE.
FROM THE PERSIAN OF KERMANI.
In Farsistan the violet spreads
Its leaves to the rival sky;
I ask how far is the Tigris flood,
And the vine that grows thereby?
Except the amber morning wind,
Not one salutes me here;
There is no lover in all Bagdat
To offer the exile cheer.
I know that thou, O morning wind!
O'er Kernan's meadow blowest,
And thou, heart-warming nightingale!
My father's orchard knowest.
The merchant hath stuffs of price,
And gems from the sea-washed strand,
And princes offer me grace
To stay in the Syrian land;
But what is gold for, but for gifts?
And dark, without love, is the day;
And all that I see in Bagdat
Is the Tigris to float me away.
FROM HAFIZ.

I said to heaven that glowed above,
O hide yon sun-filled zone,
Hide all the stars you boast;
For, in the world of love
And estimation true,
The heaped-up harvest of the moon
Is worth one barley-corn at most,
The Pleiads' sheaf but two.
If my darling should depart,
And search the skies for prouder friends,
God forbid my angry heart
In other love should seek amends.
When the blue horizon's hoop
Me a little pinches here,
Instant to my grave I stoop,
And go to find thee in the sphere.
EPITAPH.
Bethink, poor heart, what bitter kind of jest
Mad Destiny this tender stripling played;
For a warm breast of maiden to his breast,
She laid a slab of marble on his head.
They say, through patience, chalk
Becomes a ruby stone;
Ah, yes! but by the true heart's blood
The chalk is crimson grown.
FRIENDSHIP.
Thou foolish Hafiz! Say, do churls
Know the worth of Oman's pearls?
Give the gem which dims the moon
To the noblest, or to none.
Dearest, where thy shadow falls,
Beauty sits, and Music calls;
Where thy form and favour come,

All good creatures have their home.
On prince or bride no diamond stone
Half so gracious ever shone,
As the light of enterprise
Beaming from a young man's eyes.
FROM OMAR CHIAM.
Each spot where tulips prank their state
Has drunk the life-blood of the great;
The violets yon field which stain
Are moles of beauties time hath slain.
He who has a thousand friends has not a friend to spare,
And he who has one enemy will meet him everywhere.
On two days it steads not to run from thy grave,
The appointed, and the unappointed day;
On the first, neither balm nor physician can save,
Nor thee, on the second, the Universe slay.
FROM IBN JEMIN.

Two things thou shalt not long for, if thou love a mind serene;-- A woman to thy wife, though she were a crowned queen;

And the second, borrowed money,--though the smiling lender say, That he will not demand the debt until the Judgment Day.
THE FLUTE.
FROM HILALI.
Hark what, now loud, now low, the pining flute complains,
Without tongue, yellow-cheeked, full of winds that wail and sigh; Saying, Sweetheart! the old mystery remains,--
If I am I; thou, thou; or thou art I?
TO THE SHAH.
FROM HAFIZ.
Thy foes to hunt, thy enviers to strike down,
Poises Arcturus aloft morning and evening his spear.

TO THE SHAH.
FROM ENWERI.
Not in their houses stand the stars,
But o'er the pinnacles of thine!
TO THE SHAH.
FROM ENWERI.
From thy worth and weight the stars gravitate,
And the equipoise of heaven is thy house's equipoise.
SONG OF SEID NIMETOLLAH OF KUHISTAN.

[Among the religious customs of the dervishes is an astronomical dance, in which the dervish imitates the movements of the heavenly bodies, by spinning on his own axis, whilst at the same time he revolves round the Sheikh in the centre, representing the sun; and, as he spins, he sings the Song of Seid Nimetollah of Kuhistan.]

Spin the ball! I reel, I burn,
Nor head from foot can I discern,
Nor my heart from love of mine,
Nor the wine-cup from the wine.
All my doing, all my leaving,
Reaches not to my perceiving;
Lost in whirling spheres I rove,
And know only that I love.
I am seeker of the stone,
Living gem of Solomon;
From the shore of souls arrived,
In the sea of sense I dived;
But what is land, or what is wave,
To me who only jewels crave?
Love is the air-fed fire intense,
And my heart the frankincense;
As the rich aloes flames, I glow,
Yet the censer cannot know.

I'm all-knowing, yet unknowing;
Stand not, pause not, in my going.
Ask not me, as Muftis can,
To recite the Alcoran;
Well I love the meaning sweet,--
I tread the book beneath my feet.
Lo! the God's love blazes higher,
Till all difference expire.
What are Moslems? what are Giaours?
All are Love's, and all are ours.
I embrace the true believers,
But I reck not of deceivers.
Firm to Heaven my bosom clings,
Heedless of inferior things;
Down on earth there, underfoot,
What men chatter know I not.

The American essayist, lecturer, philosopher, abolitionist, and poet Ralph Waldo Emerson (May 25, 1803 – April 27, 1882), also known by his middle name Waldo, was also the founder of the transcendentalist movement in the middle of the 19th century. He was seen as a champion of individualism and a prescient critic of the countervailing pressures of society. Friedrich Nietzsche considered him "the most gifted of the Americans" and Walt Whitman referred to him as his "master".

Emerson gradually moved away from the religious and social beliefs of his contemporaries, formulating and expressing the philosophy of transcendentalism in his 1836 essay "Nature". Following this work, he gave a speech entitled "The American Scholar" in 1837, which Oliver Wendell Holmes Sr. considered to be America's "intellectual Declaration of Independence."

Emerson wrote most of his important essays as lectures first and then revised them for print. His first two collections of essays, Essays: First Series (1841) and Essays: Second Series (1844), represent the core of his thinking. They include the well-known essays "Self-Reliance", "The Over-Soul", "Circles", "The Poet", and "Experience." Together with "Nature", these essays made the decade from the mid-1830s to the mid-1840s Emerson's most fertile period. Emerson wrote on a number of subjects, never espousing fixed philosophical tenets, but developing certain ideas such as individuality, freedom, the ability for mankind to realize almost anything, and the relationship between the soul and the surrounding world. Emerson's "nature" was more philosophical than naturalistic: "Philosophically considered, the universe is composed of Nature and the Soul." Emerson is one of several figures who "took a more pantheist or pandeist approach by rejecting views of God as separate from the world."

He remains among the linchpins of the American romantic movement, and his work has greatly influenced the thinkers, writers and poets that followed him. "In all my lectures," he wrote, "I have taught one doctrine, namely, the infinitude of the private man." Emerson is also well known as a mentor and friend of Henry David Thoreau, a fellow transcendentalist.

The Rev. William Emerson, a Unitarian minister, and Ruth Haskins welcomed their son Emerson into the world on May 25, 1803, in Boston, Massachusetts. He was named after his mother's brother Ralph and his father's great-grandmother Rebecca Waldo. Ralph Waldo was the second of five sons who survived into adulthood; the others were William, Edward, Robert Bulkeley, and Charles. Three other children—Phoebe, John Clarke, and Mary Caroline—died in childhood. Emerson was entirely of English ancestry, and his family had been in New England since the early colonial period.

On May 12, 1811, less than two weeks before Emerson turned eight, his father passed away from stomach cancer. Emerson was raised by his mother, with the help of the other women in the family; his aunt Mary Moody Emerson in particular had a profound effect on him. She lived with the family off and on and maintained a constant correspondence with Emerson until her death in 1863.

When Emerson was nine years old, his formal education at the Boston Latin School began. In October 1817, at age 14, Emerson went to Harvard College and was appointed freshman messenger for the president, requiring Emerson to fetch delinquent students and send messages to faculty. Midway through his junior year, Emerson began keeping a list of books he had read and started a journal in a series of notebooks that would be called "Wide World". He took outside jobs to cover his school expenses, including as a waiter for the Junior Commons and as an occasional teacher working with his uncle Samuel and aunt Sarah Ripley in Waltham, Massachusetts. By his senior year, Emerson decided to go by his middle name, Waldo. Emerson served as Class Poet; as was custom, he presented an original poem on Harvard's Class Day, a month before his official graduation on August 29, 1821, when he was 18. He did not stand out as a student and graduated in the exact middle of his class of 59 people. In the early 1820s, Emerson was a teacher at the School for Young Ladies (which was run by his brother William). He would next spend two years living in a cabin in the Canterbury section of Roxbury, Massachusetts, where he wrote and studied nature. In his honor, this area is now called Schoolmaster Hill in Boston's Franklin Park.

Emerson sought a warmer environment in 1826 because his health was poor. He first went to Charleston, South Carolina, but found the weather was still too cold. He then went farther south, to St. Augustine, Florida, where he took long walks on the beach and began writing poetry. While in St. Augustine he made the acquaintance of Prince Achille Murat, the nephew of Napoleon Bonaparte. Murat was two years his senior; they became good friends and enjoyed each other's company. The two engaged in enlightening discussions of religion, society, philosophy, and government. Murat was a significant figure in Emerson's intellectual development, he thought.

While in St. Augustine, Emerson had his first encounter with slavery. At one point, he attended a meeting of the Bible Society while a slave auction was taking place in the yard outside. He wrote, "One ear therefore heard the glad tidings of great joy, whilst the other was regaled with 'Going, gentlemen, going!'"

After Harvard, Emerson assisted his brother William in a school for young women established in their mother's house, after he had established his own school in Chelmsford, Massachusetts; when his brother William went to Göttingen to study law in mid-1824, Ralph Waldo closed the school but continued to teach in Cambridge, Massachusetts, until early 1825. Emerson was accepted into the Harvard Divinity School in late 1824, and was inducted into Phi Beta Kappa in 1828. Emerson's brother Edward, two years younger than he, entered the office of the lawyer Daniel Webster, after graduating from Harvard first in his class. Edward's physical health began to deteriorate, and he soon suffered a mental collapse as well; he was taken to McLean Asylum in June 1828 at age 25. Although he recovered his mental equilibrium, he died in 1834, apparently from long-standing tuberculosis.

Another of Emerson's bright and promising younger brothers, Charles, born in 1808, died in 1836, also of tuberculosis, making him the third young person in Emerson's innermost circle to die in a period of a few years.

Emerson met his first wife, Ellen Louisa Tucker, in Concord, New Hampshire, on Christmas Day, 1827, and married her when she was 18 two years later. The couple moved to Boston, with Emerson's mother, Ruth, moving with them to help take care of Ellen, who was already ill with tuberculosis. Less than two years after that, on February 8, 1831, Ellen died, at the age of 20, after uttering her last words: "I have not forgotten the peace and joy". Emerson was heavily affected by her death and visited her grave in Roxbury daily. In a journal entry dated March 29, 1832, he wrote, "I visited Ellen's tomb & opened the coffin".

Boston's Second Church invited Emerson to serve as its junior pastor, and he was ordained on January 11, 1829. His initial salary was $1,200 per year (equivalent to $30,536 in 2021), increasing to $1,400 in July, but with his church role he took on other responsibilities: he was the chaplain of the Massachusetts legislature and a member of the Boston school committee. His church activities kept him busy, though during this period, facing the imminent death of his wife, he began to doubt his own beliefs.

After his wife's death, he began to disagree with the church's methods, writing in his journal in June 1832, "I have sometimes thought that, in order to be a good minister, it was necessary to leave the ministry. The profession is antiquated. In an altered age, we worship in the dead forms of our forefathers". His disagreements with church officials over the administration of the Communion service and misgivings about public prayer eventually led to his resignation in 1832. As he wrote, "This mode of commemorating Christ is not suitable to me. That is reason enough why I should abandon it". As one Emerson scholar has pointed out, "Doffing the decent black of the pastor, he was free to choose the gown of the lecturer and teacher, of the thinker not confined within the limits of an institution or a tradition".

Emerson toured Europe in 1833 and later wrote of his travels in English Traits (1856). He left aboard the brig Jasper on Christmas Day, 1832, sailing first to Malta. During his European trip, he spent several months in Italy, visiting Rome, Florence and Venice, among other cities. When in Rome, he met with John Stuart Mill, who gave him a letter of recommendation to meet Thomas Carlyle. He went to Switzerland, and had to be dragged by fellow passengers to visit Voltaire's home in Ferney, "protesting all the way upon the unworthiness of his memory". He then went on to Paris, a "loud modern New York of a place", where he visited the Jardin des Plantes. He was greatly moved by the organization of plants according to Jussieu's system of classification, and the way all such objects were related and connected. As Robert D. Richardson says, "Emerson's moment of insight into the interconnectedness of things in the Jardin des Plantes was a moment of almost visionary intensity that pointed him away from theology and toward science".

Moving north to England, Emerson met William Wordsworth, Samuel Taylor Coleridge, and Thomas Carlyle. Carlyle in particular was a strong influence on him; Emerson would later serve as an unofficial literary agent in the United States for Carlyle, and in March 1835, he tried to persuade Carlyle to come to America to lecture. The two maintained a correspondence until Carlyle's death in 1881

Emerson returned to the United States on October 9, 1833, and lived with his mother in Newton, Massachusetts. In October 1834, he moved to Concord, Massachusetts, to live with his step-grandfather, Dr. Ezra Ripley, at what was later named The Old Manse. Given the budding Lyceum movement, which provided lectures on all sorts of topics, Emerson saw a possible career as a lecturer. On November 5, 1833, he made the first of what would eventually be some 1,500 lectures, "The Uses of Natural History", in Boston. This was an expanded account of his experience in Paris.[60] In this lecture, he set out some of his important beliefs and the ideas he would later develop in his first published essay, "Nature":

Nature is a language and every new fact one learns is a new word; but it is not a language taken to pieces and dead in the dictionary, but the language put together into a most significant and universal sense. I wish to learn this language, not that I may know a new grammar, but that I may read the great book that is written in that tongue.

On January 24, 1835, Emerson wrote a letter to Lydia Jackson proposing marriage. Her acceptance reached him by mail on the 28th. In July 1835, he bought a house on the Cambridge and Concord Turnpike in Concord, Massachusetts, which he named Bush; it is now open to the public as the Ralph Waldo Emerson House. Emerson quickly became one of the leading citizens in the town. He gave a lecture to commemorate the 200th anniversary of the town of Concord on September 12, 1835. Two days later, he married Jackson in her home town of Plymouth, Massachusetts, and moved to the new home in Concord together with Emerson's mother on September 15.

Emerson quickly changed his wife's name to Lidian, and would call her Queenie,[67] and sometimes Asia, and she called him Mr. Emerson. Their children were Waldo, Ellen, Edith, and Edward Waldo Emerson. Edward Waldo Emerson was the father of Raymond Emerson. Ellen was named for his first wife, at Lidian's suggestion.

Emerson was poor when he was at Harvard, but was later able to support his family for much of his life. He inherited a fair amount of money after his first wife's death, though he had to file a lawsuit against the Tucker family in 1836 to get it. He received $11,600 in May 1834 (equivalent to $314,863 in 2021), and a further $11,674.49 in July 1837 (equivalent to $279,592 in 2021). In 1834, he considered that he had an income of $1,200 a year from the initial payment of the estate, equivalent to what he had earned as a pastor.

On September 8, 1836, the day before the publication of Nature, Emerson met with Frederic Henry Hedge, George Putnam, and George Ripley to plan periodic gatherings of other like-minded intellectuals. This was the beginning of the Transcendental Club, which served as a center for the movement. Its first official meeting was held on September 19, 1836 On September 1, 1837, women attended a meeting of the Transcendental Club for the first time. Emerson invited Margaret Fuller, Elizabeth Hoar, and Sarah Ripley for dinner at his home before the meeting to ensure that they would be present for the evening get-together. Fuller would prove to be an important figure in transcendentalism.

Emerson anonymously sent his first essay, "Nature", to James Munroe and Company to be published on September 9, 1836. A year later, on August 31, 1837, he delivered his now-famous Phi Beta Kappa address, "The American Scholar", then entitled "An Oration, Delivered before the Phi Beta Kappa Society at Cambridge"; it was renamed for a collection of essays (which included the first general publication of "Nature") in 1849. Friends urged him to publish the talk, and he did so at his own expense, in an edition of 500 copies, which sold out in a month. In the speech, Emerson declared literary independence in the United States and urged Americans to create a writing style all their own, free from Europe. James Russell Lowell, who was a student at Harvard at the time, called it "an event without former parallel on our literary annals". Another member of the audience, Reverend John Pierce, called it "an apparently incoherent and unintelligible address".

In 1837, Emerson befriended Henry David Thoreau. Though they had likely met as early as 1835, in the fall of 1837, Emerson asked Thoreau, "Do you keep a journal?" The question went on to be a lifelong inspiration for Thoreau. Emerson's own journal was published in 16 large volumes, in the definitive Harvard University Press edition issued between 1960 and 1982. Some scholars consider the journal to be Emerson's key literary work.

In March 1837, Emerson gave a series of lectures on the philosophy of history at the Masonic Temple in Boston. This was the first time he managed a lecture series on his own, and it was the beginning of his career as a lecturer. The profits from this series of lectures were much larger than when he was paid by an organization to talk, and he continued to manage his own lectures often throughout his lifetime. He eventually gave as many as 80 lectures a year, traveling across the northern United States as far as St. Louis, Des Moines, Minneapolis, and California.

On July 15, 1838, Emerson was invited to Divinity Hall, Harvard Divinity School, to deliver the school's graduation address, which came to be known as the "Divinity School Address". Emerson discounted biblical miracles and proclaimed that, while Jesus was a great man, he was not God: historical Christianity, he said, had turned Jesus into a "demigod, as the Orientals or the Greeks would describe Osiris or Apollo". His comments outraged the establishment and the general Protestant community. He was denounced as an atheist and a poisoner of young men's minds. Despite the roar of critics, he made no reply, leaving others to put forward a defense. He was not invited back to speak at Harvard for another thirty years.

The transcendental group began to publish its flagship journal, The Dial, in July 1840. They planned the journal as early as October 1839, but work did not begin until the first week of 1840. George Ripley was the managing editor. Margaret Fuller was the first editor, having been approached by Emerson after several others had declined the role. Fuller stayed on for about two years, when Emerson took over, using the journal to promote talented young writers including Ellery Channing and Thoreau.

In 1841 Emerson published Essays, his second book, which included the famous essay "Self-Reliance". His aunt called it a "strange medley of atheism and false independence", but it gained favorable reviews in London and Paris. This book, and its popular reception, more than any of Emerson's contributions to date laid the groundwork for his international fame.

In January 1842 Emerson's first son, Waldo, died of scarlet fever. Emerson wrote of his grief in the poem "Threnody" ("For this losing is true dying"), and the essay "Experience". In the same month, William James was born, and Emerson agreed to be his godfather.

Bronson Alcott announced his plans in November 1842 to find "a farm of a hundred acres in excellent condition with good buildings, a good orchard and grounds". Charles Lane purchased a 90-acre (36 ha) farm in Harvard, Massachusetts, in May 1843 for what would become Fruitlands, a community based on Utopian ideals inspired in part by transcendentalism. The farm would run based on a communal effort, using no animals for labor; its participants would eat no meat and use no wool or leather. Emerson said he felt "sad at heart" for not engaging in the experiment himself. Even so, he did not feel Fruitlands would be a success. "Their whole doctrine is spiritual", he wrote, "but they always end with saying, Give us much land and money". Even Alcott admitted he was not prepared for the difficulty in operating Fruitlands. "None of us were prepared to actualize practically the ideal life of which we dreamed. So we fell apart", he wrote. After its failure, Emerson helped buy a farm for Alcott's family in Concord which Alcott named "Hillside".

The Dial ceased publication in April 1844; Horace Greeley reported it as an end to the "most original and thoughtful periodical ever published in this country".

In 1844, Emerson published his second collection of essays, Essays: Second Series. This collection included "The Poet", "Experience", "Gifts", and an essay entitled "Nature", a different work from the 1836 essay of the same name.

Emerson made a living as a popular lecturer in New England and much of the rest of the country. He had begun lecturing in 1833; by the 1850s he was giving as many as 80 lectures per year. He addressed the Boston Society for the Diffusion of Useful Knowledge and the Gloucester Lyceum, among others. Emerson spoke on a wide variety of subjects, and many of his essays grew out of his lectures. He charged between $10 and $50 for each appearance, bringing him as much as $2,000 in a typical winter lecture season. This was more than his earnings from other sources. In some years, he earned as much as $900 for a series of six lectures, and in another, for a winter series of talks in Boston, he netted $1,600. He eventually gave some 1,500 lectures in his lifetime. His earnings allowed him to expand his property, buying 11 acres (4.5 ha) of land by Walden Pond and a few more acres in a neighboring pine grove. He wrote that he was "landlord and water lord of 14 acres, more or less".

Emerson was introduced to Indian philosophy through the works of the French philosopher Victor Cousin. In 1845, Emerson's journals show he was reading the Bhagavad Gita and Henry Thomas Colebrooke's Essays on the Vedas. He was strongly influenced by Vedanta, and much of his writing has strong shades of nondualism. One of the clearest examples of this can be found in his essay "The Over-soul":

We live in succession, in division, in parts, in particles. Meantime within man is the soul of the whole; the wise silence; the universal beauty, to which every part and particle is equally related, the eternal ONE. And this deep power in which we exist and whose beatitude is all accessible to us, is not only self-sufficing and perfect in every hour, but the act of seeing and the thing seen, the seer and the spectacle, the subject and the object, are one. We see the world piece by piece, as the sun, the moon, the animal, the tree; but the whole, of which these are shining parts, is the soul.

The central message Emerson drew from his Asian studies was that "the purpose of life was spiritual transformation and direct experience of divine power, here and now on earth."

In 1847–48, he toured the British Isles. He also visited Paris between the French Revolution of 1848 and the bloody June Days. When he arrived, he saw the stumps of trees that had been cut down to form barricades in the February riots. On May 21, he stood on the Champ de Mars in the midst of mass celebrations for concord, peace and labor. He wrote in his journal, "At the end of the year we shall take account, & see if the Revolution was worth the trees." The trip left an important imprint on Emerson's later work. His 1856 book English Traits is based largely on observations recorded in his travel journals and notebooks. Emerson later came to see the American Civil War as a "revolution" that shared common ground with the European revolutions of 1848.

In a speech in Concord, Massachusetts on May 3, 1851, Emerson denounced the Fugitive Slave Act:

The act of Congress is a law which every one of you will break on the earliest occasion—a law which no man can obey, or abet the obeying, without loss of self-respect and forfeiture of the name of gentleman.

That summer, he wrote in his diary:

This filthy enactment was made in the nineteenth century by people who could read and write. I will not obey it.

In February 1852 Emerson and James Freeman Clarke and William Henry Channing edited an edition of the works and letters of Margaret Fuller, who had died in 1850. Within a week of her death, her New York editor, Horace Greeley, suggested to Emerson that a biography of Fuller, to be called Margaret and Her Friends, be prepared quickly "before the interest excited by her sad decease has passed away". Published under the title The Memoirs of Margaret Fuller Ossoli, Fuller's words were heavily censored or rewritten. The three editors were not concerned about accuracy; they believed public interest in Fuller was temporary and that she would not survive as a historical figure. Even so, it was the best-selling biography of the decade and went through thirteen editions before the end of the century.

Walt Whitman published the innovative poetry collection Leaves of Grass in 1855 and sent a copy to Emerson for his opinion. Emerson responded positively, sending Whitman a flattering five-page letter in response. Emerson's approval helped the first edition of Leaves of Grass stir up significant interest and convinced Whitman to issue a second edition shortly thereafter. This edition quoted a phrase from Emerson's letter, printed in gold leaf on the cover: "I Greet You at the Beginning of a Great Career". Emerson took offense that this letter was made public and later was more critical of the work. Joining him were nine of the most illustrious intellectuals ever to camp out in the Adirondacks to connect with nature: Louis Agassiz, James Russell Lowell, John Holmes, Horatio Woodman, Ebenezer Rockwell Hoar, Jeffries Wyman, Estes Howe, Amos Binney, and William James Stillman. Invited, but unable to make the trip for diverse reasons, were: Oliver Wendell Holmes, Henry Wadsworth Longfellow, and Charles Eliot Norton, all members of the Saturday Club (Boston, Massachusetts).

This social club was mostly a literary membership that met the last Saturday of the month at the Boston Parker House Hotel (Omni Parker House). William James Stillman was a painter and founding editor of an art journal called the Crayon. Stillman was born and grew up in Schenectady which was just south of the Adirondack mountains. He would later travel there to paint the wilderness landscape and to fish and hunt. He would share his experiences in this wilderness to the members of the Saturday Club, raising their interest in this unknown region.

James Russell Lowell and William Stillman would lead the effort to organize a trip to the Adirondacks. They would begin their journey on August 2, 1858, traveling by train, steam boat, stagecoach, and canoe guide boats. News that these cultured men were living like "Sacs and Sioux" in the wilderness appeared in newspapers across the nation. This would become known as the "Philosophers Camp".

This event was a landmark in the nineteenth-century intellectual movement, linking nature with art and literature.

Although much has been written over many years by scholars and biographers of Emerson's life, little has been written of what has become known as the "Philosophers Camp" at Follensbee Pond. Yet, his epic poem "Adirondac" reads like a journal of his day to day detailed description of adventures in the wilderness with his fellow members of the Saturday Club. This two week camping excursion (1858 in the Adirondacks) brought him face to face with a true wilderness, something he spoke of in his essay "Nature", published in 1836. He said, "in the wilderness I find something more dear and connate than in streets or villages".

Emerson was staunchly opposed to slavery, but he did not appreciate being in the public limelight and was hesitant about lecturing on the subject. In the years leading up to the Civil War, he did give a number of lectures, however, beginning as early as November 1837. A number of his friends and family members were more active abolitionists than he, at first, but from 1844 on he more actively opposed slavery. He gave a number of speeches and lectures, and welcomed John Brown to his home during Brown's visits to Concord. He voted for Abraham Lincoln in 1860, but was disappointed that Lincoln was more concerned about preserving the Union than eliminating slavery outright. Once the American Civil War broke out, Emerson made it clear that he believed in immediate emancipation of the slaves.

Around this time, in 1860, Emerson published The Conduct of Life, his seventh collection of essays. It "grappled with some of the thorniest issues of the moment," and "his experience in the abolition ranks is a telling influence in his conclusions." In these essays Emerson strongly embraced the idea of war as a means of national rebirth: "Civil war, national bankruptcy, or revolution, [are] more rich in the central tones than languid years of prosperity."

Emerson visited Washington, D.C, at the end of January 1862. He gave a public lecture at the Smithsonian on January 31, 1862, and declared:, "The South calls slavery an institution ... I call it destitution ... Emancipation is the demand of civilization". The next day, February 1, his friend Charles Sumner took him to meet Lincoln at the White House. Lincoln was familiar with Emerson's work, having previously seen him lecture. Emerson's misgivings about Lincoln began to soften after this meeting. In 1865, he spoke at a memorial service held for Lincoln in Concord: "Old as history is, and manifold as are its tragedies, I doubt if any death has caused so much pain as this has caused, or will have caused, on its announcement." Emerson also met a number of high-ranking government officials, including Salmon P. Chase, the secretary of the treasury; Edward Bates, the attorney general; Edwin M. Stanton, the secretary of war; Gideon Welles, the secretary of the navy; and William Seward, the secretary of state.

On May 6, 1862, Emerson's protégé Henry David Thoreau died of tuberculosis at the age of 44. Emerson delivered his eulogy. He often referred to Thoreau as his best friend, despite a falling-out that began in 1849 after Thoreau published A Week on the Concord and Merrimack Rivers. Another friend, Nathaniel Hawthorne, died two years after Thoreau, in 1864. Emerson served as a pallbearer when Hawthorne was buried in Concord, as Emerson wrote, "in a pomp of sunshine and verdure".

He was elected a Fellow of the American Academy of Arts and Sciences in 1864. In 1867, he was elected as a member to the American Philosophical Society.

Starting in 1867, Emerson's health began declining; he wrote much less in his journals. Beginning as early as the summer of 1871 or in the spring of 1872, he started experiencing memory problems and suffered from aphasia. By the end of the decade, he forgot his own name at times and, if asked how he felt, would respond "Quite well; I have lost my mental faculties, but am perfectly well".

In the spring of 1871, Emerson took a trip on the transcontinental railroad, barely two years after its completion. Along the way and in California he met a number of dignitaries, including Brigham Young during a stopover in Salt Lake City. Part of his California visit included a trip to Yosemite, and while there he met a young and unknown John Muir, a signature event in Muir's career.

Emerson's Concord home caught fire on July 24, 1872. He called for help from neighbors and, giving up on putting out the flames, all tried to save as many objects as possible. The fire was put out by Ephraim Bull Jr., the one-armed son of Ephraim Wales Bull. Donations were collected by friends to help the Emersons rebuild, including $5,000 gathered by Francis Cabot Lowell, another $10,000 collected by LeBaron Russell Briggs, and a personal donation of $1,000 from George Bancroft. Support for shelter was offered as well; though the Emersons ended up staying with family at the Old Manse, invitations came from Anne Lynch Botta, James Elliot Cabot, James T. Fields and Annie Adams Fields. The fire marked an end to Emerson's serious lecturing career; from then on, he would lecture only on special occasions and only in front of familiar audiences.

While the house was being rebuilt, Emerson took a trip to England, continental Europe, and Egypt. He left on October 23, 1872, along with his daughter Ellen while his wife Lidian spent time at the Old Manse and with friends. Emerson and his daughter Ellen returned to the United States on the ship Olympus along with friend Charles Eliot Norton on April 15, 1873. Emerson's return to Concord was celebrated by the town, and school was canceled that day.

In late 1874, Emerson published an anthology of poetry entitled Parnassus, which included poems by Anna Laetitia Barbauld, Julia Caroline Dorr, Jean Ingelow, Lucy Larcom, Jones Very, as well as Thoreau and several others. Originally, the anthology had been prepared as early as the fall of 1871, but it was delayed when the publishers asked for revisions.

The problems with his memory had become embarrassing to Emerson and he ceased his public appearances by 1879. In reply to an invitation to a retirement celebration for Octavius B. Frothingham, he wrote, "I am not in condition to make visits, or take any part in conversation. Old age has rushed on me in the last year, and tied my tongue, and hid my memory, and thus made it a duty to stay at home." The New York Times quoted his reply and noted that his regrets were read aloud at the celebration. Holmes wrote of the problem saying, "Emerson is afraid to trust himself in society much, on account of the failure of his memory and the great difficulty he finds in getting the words he wants. It is painful to witness his embarrassment at times". On April 21, 1882, Emerson was found to be suffering from pneumonia. He died six days later. Emerson is buried in Sleepy Hollow Cemetery, Concord, Massachusetts. He was placed in his coffin wearing a white robe given by the American sculptor Daniel Chester French